HUGH DAVIS
AND HIS ALABAMA PLANTATION

HUGH DAVIS

and his

Alabama Plantation

by WEYMOUTH T. JORDAN

Research Professor of History
Alabama Polytechnic Institute

University, Alabama, 1948
UNIVERSITY OF ALABAMA PRESS

PREFACE

THIS STUDY is as much for the general reader as for the professional historian. It is an account of Beaver Bend, a typical cotton plantation of the Alabama blackbelt during the late ante-bellum, Civil War, and post-bellum periods. The account is long and detailed. If it seems unnecessarily so the author alone is to blame. He is the first to acknowledge that Beaver Bend was merely a representative plantation of its time and region. It is that fact, however, that seems to warrant publication of the material included here. Such detailed, personal studies as this are necessary if slavery and its accompanying plantation system and the Old South and their significance are ever to be understood properly.

Research involved in collecting materials used in this book was made possible through receipt in 1940-1941 and 1941-1942 of Southern grants-in-aid from the Social Science Research Council, for which I wish to express my deep gratitude.

In 1943, an article containing a small part of the same information included here in Chapter One was printed in the *Alabama Historical Quarterly*. I should like to thank Mrs. Marie Bankhead Owen, editor of the *Quarterly* and Director of the Alabama Department of Archives and History, for permission to reprint that material.

The study in its manuscript form was read by Dr. Alfred W. Reynolds and A. B. Metzger, both of the Department of History in the Alabama Polytechnic Institute. Their pertinent comments were consistently helpful. The editor of the Universtiy of Alabama Press, James B. McMillan, and his staff of readers have also read the manuscript and offered many excellent suggestions.

I should like to thank Mrs. E. I. Davis and her sons, Thad and N. J., of Marion, Alabama, for the use of historical collections in their possession. Most of the information presented here has come from manuscript materials that they have so thoughtfully preserved. The entire Davis family has shown me a most gracious and generous consideration, and the family and many others in the general vicinity of the Alabama blackbelt have eliminated many of the usual difficulties encountered by the student of history. Judge Irby Pope and Jesse B. Ward, officials of the Perry County Probate Court, have been especially helpful. My wife, Louise E. Jordan, has read and corrected the manuscript many times, and the study is as much hers as mine.

WEYMOUTH T. JORDAN

Alabama Polytechnic Institute
Auburn, Alabama
July, 1946

CONTENTS

MATURING OF HUGH DAVIS AND HIS REGION

BEAVER BEND was a plantation located along the Cahaba River, in Perry County, on the north central edge of the Alabama blackbelt. Its owner, Hugh Davis, moved to the little town of Marion, in Perry County, in 1834, where he practiced law for fourteen years. In 1848, he assumed the management of Beaver Bend and for the rest of his life his main interest was his plantation. At his death, in 1862, his land holdings were taken over by his sons and operated by them until the turn of the century. The residence of the elder Davis in Alabama spanned much of the period during which the region was passing from the position of the last frontier of the Old Southwest to that of a leading cotton producing state in the South before 1860. His sons were active at a time when the whole basis of their existence was giving away beneath them and also in the years when the South was attempting desperately to salvage something from the chaos resulting from the Civil War. The family is eminently worthy of notice. Its significance is that it operated, in a most typical manner, a plantation during the most important periods in the early history of Alabama and the South. More than that, the family has left behind a rather complete record of its activities.

In order to establish a proper setting for an account of the Davis family and its plantation, it is pertinent to consider very briefly the early population movements in Alabama in its formative stage and the rise to importance of the particular section of the state with which the family was intimately connected. It will be seen that the Davis's had a part in both of these developments.

It is generally agreed that the economic and social readjustments made necessary by the War of 1812 were among the chief factors which furnished the impetus for the rapid settlement of the region known at the time as the Territory of Mississippi.[1] Of practical significance, as far as this study is concerned, was the famous treaty of Fort Jackson, signed in 1815, which opened up to whites much of the Territory that was shortly to become Alabama. Almost immediately after the treaty much of the land later included in Jackson, Limestone and Lauderdale Counties was settled; and before the close of 1815 those areas were attracting many home seekers. Some wealthy planters also began establishing large enterprises in Madison County, while others took up land in the lower Tombigbee River Valley region. While the population figure for the settled areas of Alabama (then the eastern half of the Territory of Mississippi) had amounted to approximately thirteen thousand just before the treaty of Fort Jackson, the figure increased to more than twenty-five thousand in 1816. By March, 1817, when the Territory of Alabama was created by the United States Congress, the white population had passed the thirty-three thousand mark. The important settled areas, too, had increased in number. Besides the older settlements in the Tennessee River Valley and on the lower Tombigbee River, people had also moved to the upper Tombigbee as well as to the Mobile River Valley. Indeed, South Alabama had become the more densely settled area, and more

[1]The following are among those books examined by the author to obtain information on the early developments in Alabama: Charles S. Davis, *The Cotton Kingdom in Alabama* (Montgomery, 1939); Albert James Pickett, *The History of Alabama, . . .* (Sheffield, Alabama, 1896); Charles S. Sydnor, *Benjamin L. C. Wailes, A Gentleman of the Old Natchez Region* (Durham, 1938); Peter J. Hamilton, *Colonial Mobile* (Boston, 1897); Thomas M. Owen, *History of Alabama and Dictionary of Alabama Biography*, 4 vols. (Chicago, 1921); Marcus L. Hansen, "The Population of American Outlying Regions in 1790," in American Historical Association, *Annual Report, 1931,* I (Washington, 1932); Thomas Perkins Abernethy, *The Formative Period in Alabama, 1815-1828* (Montgomery, 1922); E. C. Betts, *Early History of Huntsville, Alabama* (Montgomery, 1916); John W. Monette, *History of the Discovery and Settlement of the Valley of the Mississippi*, 2 vols. (New York, 1846); Albert B. Moore, *History of Alabama and Her People*, 3 vols. (Chicago and New York, 1927); Ulrich B. Phillips, *History of Transportation in the Eastern Cotton Belt to 1860* (New York, 1908); *Statutes at Large;* and Kendric Charles Babcock, *The Rise of American Nationality, 1811-1819* (New York, 1906).

than half of the settlers were living in Mobile, Baldwin, Washington, and Clark Counties. Two years later, when Alabama became a state, its total inhabitants had increased to more than seventy thousand. In 1820, the total population was above 127,000.[2]

Meanwhile, some of the land in the region now comprising Perry County, Alabama, was also being taken up by intrepid settlers.[3] In December, 1816, a trader named Anderson West, who was perhaps the first white man to settle in the region today included in Perry County, built a log cabin near a place known as Cahaba Old Town, located at a point about seven miles northeast of the present location of the town of Marion. In the next few years many settlers followed West to the area, and in March, 1822, the locality later to be known as Marion was selected as the seat of government for Perry County. At the time Marion contained only one family. Shortly afterwards, however, there were signs of activity in the vicinity. In June, 1822, a church, the Siloam Baptist which still functions, was organized, and within the next few months three taverns were opened for business.[4] From its meager beginnings Marion slowly developed within the next ten years into a trade center for its county and region. But as late as the year 1830, it was still not much to behold, for it was later described as being in that year a "delapidated Sleepy town, with dingy houses."[5] No newspaper was yet published in the county seat, although newspapers had been in print in Cahaba and Greensboro,[6] nearby towns, as early as 1826 and 1827. Tree stumps had been only partially removed from the town streets. The business group, shortly to be greatly augmented, amounted in 1830 only to three tavern-keepers, one bar-keeper, three merchants, three physicians, four lawyers, one carpenter, one cabinet-maker, one tailor, and one Negro blacksmith.[7]

Although Marion in 1830 was not yet important economically or

[2]*Niles' Weekly Register*, XLVI (Baltimore, Aug. 16, 1834), 424, states that Alabama's population was 127,901 in 1820, and 309,527 in 1830.

[3]An early settler in Perry County was a person named Captain W. L. Fagin, who, in 1886, had published a history of Marion and Perry County in the local newspaper, *The Marion Standard*. Later, in 1909, reprints of his account appeared in the same newspaper. It is from this latter source that much of the information of the early developments in Marion has been obtained.

[4]*The Marion Standard*, Apr. 2, 1909.

[5]*Ibid.*, Mar. 26, 1909.

[6]For an account of early Cahaba, see Anna M. Gayle Fry, *Memories of Old Cahaba* (Nashville, 1905), *passim*.

[7]*The Marion Standard*, Mar. 26, 1909. A good general description of Marion's early history appears in S. A. Townes, *The History of Marion, Sketches of Life, etc. in Perry*

socially, the state of Alabama as a whole was making great progress. Since 1820, the state's population had increased from about 127,000 to more than 300,000.[8] The river valleys in South Alabama had established themselves as the chief cotton growing areas of the state.[9] Mobile, at the mouth of the Alabama and Tombigbee River systems, was already attracting wide attention as a cotton port, and by 1830 had a population of 3,194.[10] In the early 1830's, however, Marion also entered the years of its greatest boom period. The town owed its importance to the development of the cultivation of cotton as the chief occupation of the people who lived in the immediate vicinity. Its prosperity came primarily as a result of the final realization that the soil of the adjacent blackbelt was extraordinarily adaptable for the cultivation of cotton, especially of an upland, blight-proof variety of the staple which had just been introduced in the region. Agriculturists in Perry County and other parts of Alabama were at last convinced that the sticky, messy blackbelt soil and reputedly unhealthy area could be turned to their advantage.[11] The ultimate result was the rise of Alabama to the position of a foremost cotton producing state in the South. With this all-absorbing interest and activity came many new customs, great wealth, a highly developed social order, many social problems, uncompromising support of the institution of slavery, and finally, in an effort to maintain the social and economic system which had developed from the production of cotton, a willingness to go to war.

Evidence of the boom in Marion is the amount of land which was taken up in the blackbelt section of Perry County. As it happens there are only five territorial sub-divisions of the county which are completely within the blackbelt.[12] They contain a total of 180 irregular sections

County, Alabama (Marion, 1844), *passim.* See also Weymouth T. Jordan, "Early Ante-bellum Marion, Alabama: A Black Belt Town," *The Alabama Historical Quarterly,* V (Spring Issue, 1943), 12-31, and the same author's "The Elisha F. King Family: Planters of the Alabama Black Belt," *Agricultural History,* XIX (July, 1945), 152-162.

[8]*Niles' Weekly Register,* XLVI (Baltimore, Aug. 16, 1834), 424.

[9]South Alabama produced 7,000 bales of cotton in 1818; 16,000 in 1820; 58,283 in 1825; and 102,684 in 1830. *Mobile Shipping and Commercial List,* Oct. 3, 1835, and *Mobile Journal of Commerce Letter-Sheet Price-Current,* Sept. 1, 1851, in William A. Jones Papers (in possession of Miss Emma Jones and Mrs. Mary J. Lowery, Perry County, Alabama). Cited hereafter as Jones Papers.

[10]*Fifteenth Census of the United States: Population* (Washington, 1931), I, 66.

[11]See Abernethy, *op. cit.,* 57-58.

[12]These sub-divisions are: township eighteen, north, ranges six, seven and eight, east;

of land, comprising 112,565½ acres.[13] Most of this blackbelt region
was purchased after 1830, with the amazing total of 91,394 acres being
purchased from 1830 through 1835. In 1830 alone the amount entered at the land office at Cahaba was 31,128 acres.[14] After 1835, the
rest of the blackbelt soil was purchased intermittently until 1852, and at
the end of the latter year all of the land was privately owned, except
the few acres still held by the state for educational purposes.[15]

Perhaps the results locally of the final appreciation of the Perry
County blackbelt in the early 1830's is best described by the following
quotation from a "Conversation with an Old Settler": "I came to Perry
County in 1832 with Anderson West, who was speculating in Negroes,
and brought a drove with him at the time. Passing through the Creek
Indians, we camped at Mt. Meigs, west [sic] of Montgomery. Farmers
were picking cotton and clearing land,—the axes were cutting until
midnight, and an hour before day next morning. Camped near Marion
Saturday night. Negroes were cutting timber all night until sunrise
Sunday. Marion was thronged with people on Sunday, talking about
cotton and 'niggers.' Every man we met, either wanted to buy a
'nigger' or take a drink."[16] Great changes indeed took place in the
social and economic life of Perry County and the blackbelt from the
thirties until the outbreak of the Civil War. As a whole Alabama
prospered during the period because of the cotton economy developing
there in those years. Population, white and black, increased enormous-
ly. Important towns sprang up. Transportation facilities, mainly
for the purpose of moving cotton speedily, were augmented.[17] Of
particular importance of course was the spectacular climb in the output
of cotton; and Marion was among the towns to benefit from the new
interest. Perry County was in the middle of the cotton country, and

township seventeen, north, range six, east; and township sixteen, north, range six, east.
[13]Alabama Tract Book, Perry County (Office of Probate Court, Courthouse, Marion),
pp. 1-36, 97-108, 151-162.
[14]Land to the amount of 11,304 acres was bought in 1831; 14,711 in 1832; 9,212 in
1833; 13,379 in 1834; and 11,657 in 1835. *Ibid.*
[15]Entries were made for 1,510 acres in 1836; 199 in 1837; none in 1838 and 1839;
40 in 1840; 40 in 1841; none in 1842 and 1843; 40 in 1844; 280 in 1845; 39 in 1846;
919 in 1847; 161 in 1848; 359 in 1849; 80 in 1850; none in 1851; and 80 in 1852. *Ibid.*
[16]*The Marion Standard*, Apr. 9, 1909.
[17]For contemporary descriptions of Alabama written by several English and Scotch
travellers who toured the state in the 1830's, see Thomas Hamilton, *Men and Manners
in America*, 2 vols. (London, 1833), II, 240, and Walter Brownlow Posey (ed.), "Alabama in the 1830's As Recorded by British Travellers," in Birmingham-Southern College
Bulletin, XXXI (December, 1938), *passim.*

Marion was not only the county seat but became also a trade center for some of the largest planters of the state. The town and the general region in which it was situated attracted many new settlers in the thirties, and the blackbelt area began an era of good times which continued, except for the nation-wide Panic of 1837, until the outbreak of war in 1861.[18]

Marion became a center of extensive legal transactions resulting from the almost unending purchase and sale of slaves and land. To take care of the increase in legal business and litigations, many lawyers moved into the bustling little town. Among the members of the profession who were attracted to Marion was a young man by the name of Hugh Davis, who, as far as can be ascertained, arrived in Marion in December, 1834.[19] At about the same time two of his brothers moved to other towns in the Alabama blackbelt. One, also a lawyer, settled for a short time in Eutaw, in Greene County. The other, a physician, moved to Greensboro, then in Greene County, and now the seat of Hale County. He remained in Greensboro for a few years, then moved to Citronelle, a small place in South Alabama.[20]

It will be seen that in moving to Alabama, Hugh Davis and his family went by a round-about route followed by many of their contemporaries. His great-grandfather, William Davis, a son of a Sir John Davis of Glenmore Shire, Wales, had emigrated to Virginia early in the eighteenth century. One of William Davis' sons, Stephen, had taken up land in Hanover County, Virginia, where he had become a successful planter. Shortly after the American Revolution, Stephen, following the example of thousands of persons living in the seaboard states of the Upper South, had moved westward in order to enter some of the cheap land which became available at the close of the war. Dur-

[18]The following official records of Perry County, on deposit in the Office of Probate Court, Courthouse, Marion, contain pertinent information about the early developments in the county and in Marion: Perry County, Record Book (Feb., 1820-Oct., 1840), pp. 1-152, 155, 230, 255, 259, 260, 266, 268, 280, 294, 295, 304, 320, 341, 378; Perry County, Orphan's Court Register, A, 2, 3, 8, 9-12, 43, 44, 56, 62, 67, 68, 101, 131; Perry County, Minutes, Orphan's Court, A, 18, 20, 58, 88, 103, 105, 107; *ibid*, B, 171.

[19]*The Marion Commonwealth*, June ?, 1862. Under the date of November 30, 1854, Davis wrote in his Farm Book or Diary, that he had been in Perry County for twenty years. This Farm Book (in possession of Mrs. L. I. Davis and sons, Thad and N. J., all of Perry County) is cited hereafter as Farm Book.

[20]John C. Thompson to Hugh Davis, Aug. 18, 1845, and Stephen Davis to Hugh Davis, July 15, 1856, in Hugh Davis Papers (in possession of Mrs. L. I. Davis and sons). Cited hereafter as Davis Papers.

ing the late colonial period, land to the west of the Middle Atlantic English colonies had changed hands numerous times among speculators who lived in Virginia, the Carolinas, and other colonies. After 1781, following the well-known vicissitudes of the controversies over land claims, much of the region in the West passed into the hands of the Confederation Government. A few years after Yorktown the western lands, in part, were opened to settlement, and among the Virginians going to the West was Stephen Davis. Like his contemporaries, in migrating he was probably seeking a better life based on the acquisition of cheap land, and in moving he was merely joining in a general exodus from East to West.[21] Although not much is known about his activities either in Virginia or in his new home, it is known that by 1787 he had established residence near Lexington, in Fayette County, which was shortly to become part of the state of Kentucky when that commonwealth was admitted to the Union in 1792. The only other information learned about him is that he remained in Kentucky the rest of his life, that he raised a large family, and that he became a planter.[22]

After a generation in Kentucky several members of the Davis family left their home to participate in another general migration. This time they partook in a trek to the south, into the Territory of Mississippi, which had been established in 1798. As already mentioned, this movement within the South, as well as one of the same period to the southwestward from the seaboard states of the Upper South, was in progress during and immediately after the War of 1812 with England. Just as the elder Davis had left Virginia for the purpose of acquiring cheap land in Kentucky his son, Nathaniel Bowe Davis,[23] moved southward in order to obtain low-priced land in the Mississippi Territory. Since its establishment the Territory had gained greatly both in population and commercial importance.[24] The younger Davis arrived in the

[21]For a full account of this westward movement, see Thomas Perkins Abernethy, *Western Lands and the American Revolution* (New York, 1937), *passim*. Frank L. Owsley, "The Pattern of Migration and Settlement on the Southern Frontier," *Journal of Southern History*, XI (May, 1945), 147-176, contains significant information on the settlement of Alabama and other states of the Lower South. See also William O. Lynch, "The Westward Flow of Southern Colonists Before 1861," in *ibid.*, X (August, 1943), 303-327.

[22]Information concerning the migrations of the Davis family has been furnished by Mrs. L. I. Davis. See also *The Montgomery* (Alabama) *Advertiser*, June 11, 1905, which contains an annotated genealogy of the family.

[23]Nathaniel Bowe Davis was born on June 19, 1784, according to Farm Book, June 19, 1857.

[24]Sydnor, *op. cit.*, pp. 3-91, contains a summary of the early developments in the

eastern section of the Territory early in 1817 and took up land at a locality about seventeen miles northwest of Huntsville.[25] In going to that region of the Territory he of course picked out one of the most popular areas within Mississippi. He had barely settled down, however, before the section to which he had moved was included within the boundaries of the newly created Alabama Territory. For some reason he became dissatisfied in his new home, and a few years after establishing himself near Huntsville he moved a second time. He left Alabama for a plantation which he had acquired near DeSoto, Mississippi, and for the rest of his life made his home there.[26]

Before leaving Kentucky, Nathaniel Bowe Davis had married and, similar to his father, had a large family. His son, Hugh, with whom this study is primarily concerned, was born on November 22, 1811.[27] Thus Hugh was only five years of age when his family moved from Kentucky to its new establishment near Huntsville. He was of course only a few years older when the family left Alabama for Mississippi. He must have led the typical life of a young boy and of a youth on a Deep South cotton plantation of his day. He probably saw a plantation developed from a wilderness, and no doubt took some part in the work involed in the task. No information is available concerning his years in Mississippi; and only assumptions may be made in regard to his education. It is very probable that he attended schools operated by private teachers, since such schooling was the usual kind for boys of his class of society. Moreover, in later life he demonstrated personal interests of a type which are usually developed especially by persons possessing at least some formal educational training. When he moved to Marion, in 1834, he was only twenty-three years of age, and had already prepared himself as a lawyer. His two brothers who moved to the Alabama blackbelt were also professional men. Still another brother remained in Mississippi and became a lawyer in the town of Hernando.[28]

Within a few years after his arrival in Marion, Hugh Davis had built up a most respectable law practice. In the beginning he and other lawyers there gave their attention "more particularly to the settlement

Territory of Mississippi.
[25]*The Montgomery Advertiser*, June 11, 1905.
[26]*Ibid.*; Nathaniel Bowe Davis died in 1857. Farm Book, Nov. 22, 1857.
[27]Farm Book, Nov. 22, 1851.
[28]James R. Davis to Hugh Davis, Dec. 14, 1851, in Davis Papers.

of estates, which at the time was the most lucrative branch of practice."[29]
At the same time, one of the most significant factors in his success in
Marion was his marriage, in 1840,[30] to a daughter of Thomas Anderson
Jones, of Dallas and Perry Counties. The marriage in itself indicates,
perhaps more than any other accomplishment, that he had within a few
years attained a highly respected social position in his adopted home.
The background of the Jones family was exceptionally good, as was
that of Davis' own family. Ancestors of Davis' wife had emigrated
in the early colonial period from France to America, where they had
settled and become successful planters in Virginia and in the Carolinas. Early in the nineteenth century, Thomas Anderson Jones left
his plantation in Mecklenburg County, Virginia, and moved to Madison County, in what later became North Alabama. In the 1820's he
had moved again, this time for the purpose of opening up a plantation
in Perry and Dallas Counties.[31] After his marriage Davis built a town
house in Marion,[32] and lived there as long as he maintained a law office, that is, until December, 1851. Partially because of the contacts
afforded by his excellent marriage, as well as the ability demonstrated
in the conduct of his practice, he acquired a wide reputation and became one of the most sought after lawyers in central Alabama. His
obituary, published in 1862 in a Marion newspaper, states that after
his arrival in Perry County he "soon became a leading and respected
member of the community and of the legal profession."[33]

Davis moved to Marion at an opportune time. Perry County was
enjoying great prosperity and, moreover, was receiving wide attention
because of its lucrative agricultural activity. Even the popular periodi-
cal, *Niles' Weekly Register,* of Baltimore, Maryland, under the date
line of October 17, 1835, carried the following account:

We learn from *Marion, Alabama,* that—The crops of this county [Perry] are exceedingly promising, notwithstanding the loud and *usual* complaints of the planters.
True, those living on the prairies and cane brakes have suffered much from the rot,
and those on the sandy lands, a little by the insects, but we presume that no one will
deny that this is not a much better average crop than that of last year; and that a man
must be a miser and an ingrate, who would not be satisfied with such a reward of his
labor as was yielded last year; . . .

[29]*The Marion Standard,* Mar. 19, 1909.
[30]Farm Book, Dec. 18, 1857.
[31]Jones Papers.
[32]Memoranda, dated Jan. 2, 1844, and Mar. 12, 1845, in Davis Papers.
[33]*The Marion Commonwealth,* June ?, 1862.

Production of cotton in the state as a whole more than tripled between 1830 and 1840, mainly as a result of the extraordinary and spectacular increase in the blackbelt and South Alabama.[34] In the latter region the total annual bales sky-rocketed from 102,684 in 1830 to 445,725 in 1840.[35] The entire state naturally profited from the cotton crops, the importance of the blackbelt was especially enhanced, and towns such as Marion prospered more than at any time in their history. The huge production of cotton was continued in the forties. Mobile, the port which handled practically all cotton made in the Alabama blackbelt, jumped in population from 3,194 in 1830 to 12,672 in 1840.[36] From the city the amazing total of 4,230,730 bales of cotton, most of it produced in Alabama, was shipped between 1841 and 1851.[37]

When Davis arrived in Marion in 1834, the town had become the terminus of at least two stage coach lines. Contact by water was well established with towns located along the Alabama River system, most local commercial contacts being with Cahaba and Selma, in Dallas County, and with Mobile. The Marion people had access to information of all sorts from the outside, and although the town itself still had no newspaper its citizens subscribed to papers printed elsewhere. Among the state newspapers being read in 1834 were *The* (Cahaba) *Alabama Republican;* the *Selma Free Press;* and the *States Rights Expositor and Spirit of the Age* of Tuscaloosa, Alabama.[38] Many out-of-state publications were circulated, one of the significant characteristics of the people of the agricultural South of the period being that of sub-

[34]An "Abstract of the Returns of the Fifth Census," in *Niles' Weekly Register,* XLIII (Baltimore, Sept. 15, 1832), 35, lists the following counties as those located in South Alabama in 1830: Mobile, Monroe, Baldwin, Dallas, Pickens, Bibb, Montgomery, Clark, Shelby, Butler, Henry, Marengo, Greene, Pike, Perry, Conecuh, Autauga, Wilcox, Dale, Fayette, Covington, Washington, Lowndes, and Tuscaloosa. Counties listed in the same "Abstract" as comprising North Alabama in 1830, were: Madison, Limestone, Jefferson, Walker, Marion, Morgan, St. Clair, Lawrence, Franklin, Lauderdale, Blount, and Jackson.

[35]*Mobile Shipping and Commercial List,* Oct. 3, 1835, in Jones Papers; (Mobile) *Register Shipping List and Prices-Current,* Dec. 7, 1839; *Mobile Journal of Commerce Letter-Sheet Price-Current,* Sept. 1, 1851, in Elisha F. King Papers (in possession of Miss Clara Barker, Marion). Cited hereafter as King Papers.

[36]*Fifteenth Census of the United States: Population* (Washington. 1931), I, 66.

[37]*Mobile Shipping and Commercial List,* Oct. 3, 1835; (Mobile) *Register Shipping List and Prices-Current,* Dec. 7, 1839; *Mobile Journal of Commerce Letter-Sheet Price Current,* Sept. 1, 1851; in King Papers. Charles S. Davis, *The Cotton Kingdom in Alabama,* p. 42, states that 564,429 bales of cotton were produced in Alabama in 1850.

[38]Perry County, Minutes, Orphan's Court, A, 279; *ibid.,* B, 40, 72, 139.

scribing to numerous newspapers, periodicals and printed materials of all kinds.

Among the outstanding accomplishments of the people of Marion in the 1830's was the establishment of several institutions of higher learning. In 1832 no schools, except a few private ones, existed. But within ten years Marion boasted of three colleges, two for women and one for men. The first institution to open its doors was the Marion Female Seminary, a Methodist school which was organized in 1836. The school never had a large attendance but did continue to operate as late as 1918. The other school set up for women was the Judson Female Institute, which soon became a Baptist institution and subsequently had its name changed to Judson College. It was founded in 1838 and still functions in Marion. The third school to be established was Howard College for men. After much consideration it was set up in 1842 and continued to operate in Marion until 1887-1888, when it was moved to Birmingham, Alabama, where it is today.[39] By 1842, with its three schools, Marion could correctly be considered as a center of education in Alabama.

There is no doubt that the presence of the colleges in Marion brought about a social advance as important as the economic. Teachers from all sections of the country, and even from Europe, moved to Marion and took with them new ideas and conceptions. Many novel social habits were introduced and the teachers and the schools were partially responsible for speeding up the general cultural development of the region in which they were located.[40] With three colleges in the neighborhood, the people of Perry County could attend numerous public receptions, speeches, concerts, and similar functions. Social affairs of all kinds were held frequently, and to them went the people of the region. On one occasion in 1847, for example, a Marion matron wrote to her husband who was at the time on a visit to New York City that "The Judson concert came off on last Thursday

[39]Townes, *op. cit.*, pp. 15, 52, 60; Louise Manly, *History of Judson College* (Atlanta, 1899), p. 9; *Howard College Bulletin*, XCVIII (Birmingham, 1940), 22; *Judson Catalogue, 1844-1861, passim*; A. Elizabeth Taylor, "Regulations Governing Life at the Judson Female Institute During the Decade Preceding the Civil War," *The Alabama Historical Quarterly*, III (Spring Issue, 1941), 23-29.

[40]For a partial discussion of this idea, in another locality, see F. Garvin Davenport, "Culture Versus Frontier in Tennessee, 1825-1850," *Journal of Southern History*, V (February, 1939), 18-33.

evening and was very well attended as the Judson concerts always are. . . ."[41]

Meanwhile, many noticeable physical changes had occurred in Marion. By 1844 the place comprised one square mile and had a population of 1500.[42] Numerous new business concerns had been organized and in 1844 a resident described them as follows: "We have eight dry goods stores, which all together sell annually, say $180,000, according to the estimate of one of our intelligent merchants. Marion has also two groceries—not dram shops—two confectionaries; two drug stores, two shoe makers' shops, one tin ware manufactory, two saddlers shops, two livery stables, three blacksmiths' shops, four tailors' shops, two carriage makers, one gin factory, two cabinet work shops, two printing offices—the Marion Telegraph office . . . and the Herald office . . . and the Independent Order of Odd Fellows, have opened a lodge. . . ."[43] The Masonic Order also had a lodge in town. Professional men were listed as "9 Preachers, 6 Doctors of Medicine, M. D., 3 Botanic or Steam Doctors, 15 Lawyers, 2 Resident Surgeon Dentists, 1 Barber."[44] In 1844, church memberships were: Baptist, 375; Presbyterian, 213; Methodist, 78; and Campbellites, 15. An Episcopal Church was also in operation and the Latter Day Saints claimed a small membership in Marion.[45] A temperance society had about five hundred members. So-called Whig and Democratic discussion groups had been organized, and at their meetings were talking about the expediency of a national bank, the Quadruple Alliance, the Holy Alliance, "and other such small matters."[46] Marion in 1844 was indeed very much alive.

In such a community, a center of trade, education and county government, located in one of the country's richest agricultural regions, a competent lawyer could confidently expect to make a good living. It was Hugh Davis' fortune to do just that from 1834 to 1852. His first problems of course were to attract attention to himself and business to his office, but both were soon accomplished. His marriage

[41]Mary A. Fowlkes to Samuel H. Fowlkes, Mar. 1, 1847 (in possession of Edward Lee, Sylacauga, Alabama). Cited hereafter as Fowlkes Papers.

[42]Townes, *op. cit.*, p. 30.

[43]*Ibid.*, pp. 33-34.

[44]*Ibid.*, p. 33.

[45]*Ibid.*, p. 32. See Mormon Bible on deposit in Perry County courthouse.

[46]*Ibid.*, p. 26; Perry County, Minutes, Commissioners Court (Office of Probate Court, Courthouse, Marion), A, 57; B, 20.

into a family of first-rate local importance helped much in both respects. Probably of equal significance, however, was his service on
various local committees appointed by the County Commissioners
Court. He became a member of several committees appointed to select
routes for the roads being constructed in the county. For several years
he was a school commissioner in one of the townships of the county.[47]
For a time he sat on a committee of three charged with the function
of maintaining a check on the expenditure of Perry County funds. He
saw service, too, as an apportioner of hands to work the county roads.[48]
At least for five years during the 1840's he was County Solicitor, and
in this position attended to the legal affairs of the local government
and represented it in all cases before the local courts.

During part of his legal practice in Marion, especially from 1842
to 1852, Davis was the local representative of several Alabama banking
establishments. He was particularly active in conducting the affairs
in Marion and Perry County for the State Bank of Alabama. In
this work his duties had to do primarily with the collection of debts
owed to the Bank, and usually with loans and mortgages which had
been incurred by blackbelt planters in their extensive purchases of
Negroes and land.[49] He also had the legal problem of untangling
claims which the Bank had obtained to land located in central Alabama, and this task often meant that he had to travel from one end
of the state to the other. His relations with the Bank must have been
quite satisfactory, for in 1845 he received a note from the president of
the main branch at Tuscaloosa stating that "we are well pleased with
your exertions and energy as local Attorney."[50] The position brought
him recognition and some wealth, his annual stipend amounting to five
hundred dollars plus a commission of $2\frac{1}{2}\%$ on all collections made.[51]

For several years he was also attorney for the Cahaba and Marion

[47]In 1851, the principal of the Centenary Institute, of Summerfield, Alabama, in-
vited Davis to serve as "a member of the Visiting Committee to attend the annual
examination of the pupils of said Institute." B. J. Harrison to Davis, Apr. 27, 1851,
in Davis Papers.

[48]Perry County, Record Book, 360; Perry County, Minutes, Commissioners Court,
A, 48, 223; B, 53.

[49]For a Virginian's surprise at the great extravagance and optimism of certain planters
in the Alabama blackbelt, see Herbert A. Kellar (ed), "A Journey Through the South
in 1836: Diary of James D. Davidson," *Journal of Southern History,* I (August, 1935),
365-367.

[50]Arthur Foster to Davis, Nov. 26, 1845, in Davis Papers.

[51]Statement of Jan., 1842, in *ibid.*

Railroad, a company organized in the 1830's. The position never brought in large fees, but, similar to the attorneyship for the State Bank, it afforded many valuable contacts. Unfortunately for Davis' fees he was connected with the railroad at the time when it was strained with construction costs, and his important task seems to have been that of keeping the creditors of the company satisfied. In January, 1848, the railroad had ninety-nine stockholders, owning shares amounting to $68,600. But all available money had been expended on construction, and the shareholders agreed to raise additional funds "by a further sale of stock."[52] Immediately afterwards, the company was successful in selling new bonds, and construction was continued. At long last, in the summer of 1857, the railroad was completed from Cahaba to Marion. Because of its connection with the Alabama River at Cahaba, the railroad immediately became popular with the Perry County planters. For the remainder of the ante-bellum period it was one of their chief transportation outlets.[53] As for Hugh Davis, it has been impossible to ascertain his precise connection with the railroad after January, 1848. He did, however, attend meetings of the Board of Directors as late as January 30, 1854.[54] But by the latter date he had given up his law practice and it is assumed that he attended the meetings as a stockholder.

Meanwhile, Davis had continued his law practice. From 1834 to 1852, he was retained as legal representative of numerous planters in Perry County. His fees brought in rather large sums of money, one planter paying $856.00 for services rendered in one year.[55] He frequently received inquiries from leading merchant houses over the country requesting information concerning prospective customers. Collection agencies and merchants located in New York City, Boston, Philadelphia, Charleston, Savannah, Mobile and New Orleans retained

[52]List of Shareholders and Stock Owned, in *ibid.*; W. W. Fambro to Davis, Jan. 31, 1848, in *ibid.*; Official Report of John Lockhart, Treasurer of the Cahaba and Marion Railroad, in *ibid.*

[53]Edwin W. King Diary, Sept. 24, 1853 (in possession of Mrs. Leta B. Hart, Marion), cited hereafter as King Diary; see also *Judson Institute Catalogue* (Marion, 1857), p. 25, and Albert Burton Moore, *History of Alabama* (University, Alabama, 1934), pp. 313, 314. Information on Alabama railroads in the ante-bellum period may also be found in Davis, *The Cotton Kingdom in Alabama*, pp. 118, 131-132. See also Albert B. Moore, "Railroad Building in Alabama During Reconstruction," *Journal of Southern History*, I (November, 1935), 421-441.

[54]Farm Book, Jan. 30, 1854.

[55]Statement, of unknown date, in Davis Papers.

him as their agent in central Alabama.[56] By 1848, however, he had reached a turning point in his life, and at that time decided to shift his activities from his law office to the operation of a cotton plantation. In other words, he lived a life which was typical of many men of the South of his day. He was the grand-son of a planter who had crossed the mountains from Virginia into Kentucky; his father had followed a general trend by moving southward from Kentucky to Mississippi; Davis himself became a lawyer; and after a successful practice was ready, in 1848, to turn to what he probably considered to be the most desirable life of a Southern gentleman—operation of a cotton plantation located in the Southern blackbelt. The cycle was complete. More than that, he worked at the job of planting at a period in his state's history when such an occupation was one of the most important features of the economic order of Alabama.

During the 1840's, while serving as County Solicitor, it was Davis' good fortune to be in a position to learn first-hand of impending sales of land for taxes or for other reasons. He thus often had ample opportunities to bid in land when it came up for sale, and in this manner he acquired hundreds of acres of land which he no doubt planned from the beginning to operate as a plantation. Some land was also obtained by outright purchases, and by the time he was thirty-eight years of age he had rather extensive land holdings. His first purchase of farm land in Perry County was made in October, 1841, and during the next nine years he obtained all the land he could afford. Most of it was located along the Cahaba River, at a point about ten miles southeast of Marion. By April, 1847, he owned 1,270 acres;[57] in December, 1848, he had 3,662 acres, with which he began his plantation; and by November, 1850, his holdings had increased to 5,462 acres.[58]

This last figure represents the largest number of acres Davis ever owned at one time and it was the land he used during most of his career as a planter, although it should be noted particularly that he never had as many as one thousand acres under cultivation at any one time. He called his place Beaver Bend Plantation because it was lo-

[56]Davis Papers.
[57]*Ibid.*; Perry County, Alabama, Deed Record (Office of Probate Court, Marion), F, 110, 447, 513, 560, 623; G, 78, 82, 588; H, 296.
[58]*Ibid.*, E, 22, 261, 263; F, 110, 264, 265, 447, 495, 513, 559, 560, 623; G, 27, 78, 82, 496, 513, 556, 559, 588, 631, 676, 732, 761; H, 191, 296, 413, 414, 416, 439, 505, 603, 613, 618; I, 20, 137, 143, 203, 340, 444, 460, 498, 550, 596, 618; K, 199, 453, 474; L, 415; M, 28; N, 245, 246, 539; O, 137, 160, 266.

cated at a point on the Cahaba River which he designated as Beaver's Bend. Similar to other planters, he bought much of his land on credit,[59] but it is worthy of note that he knew when to quit adding to his holdings and that all of his dealings after November, 1850, involved town lots owned in Marion.[60] It may be observed, too, that his realization that he had enough farm land for his purposes was in keeping with his conservative nature. He was never a person to act prematurely and was judicious and even methodical in all of his financial transactions, except in his purchases of slaves. Even after beginning to operate his plantation he waited four years before definitely giving up his law practice. He started managing Beaver Bend in January, 1848, but continued to live in Marion until December, 1851. On December 18 of the latter year he recorded in his farm book, "Family moved down to remain permanently on plantation, if planting is agreeable." On the last day of the year, he and a few of his slaves "Went to Marion . . . & brought down furniture."[61] A year later he was of the opinion: "Farming is a fine business for a man that can't do anything else."[62]

Before and after becoming a planter, Davis was in most respects representative of the men of his class, and he seems to have taken full advantage of the cultural attributes of his region. His daughters attended the Marion Female Seminary and his sons enrolled at Howard College and at the University of Alabama, the latter school having been established in the town of Tuscaloosa. Davis himself always showed great interest in the Marion schools and often made subscriptions to them.[63] He never gave his financial support to the Judson Institute, however, probably because his father-in-law was closely as-

---

[59]On October 2, 1847, Davis bought 437 acres of land and paid $1,311, the first of three annual installments, on the purchase. At about the same time he bought the same number of acres from another person and agreed to make three annual payments of $1,666.66 for the land. Payments were not made on time, however. Receipts, in Davis Papers; Farm Book, Jan. 1, 1848.

[60]On January 1, 1853, Davis obtained $2,000 cash for a store lot in Marion; on February 6, 1853, he sold another lot for $1,000 cash. Farm Book, Jan. 1, Feb. 6, 1853. For sales of other town lots, see Perry County, Deed Record, K, 199, 453, 474; L, 415; M, 28; N, 245, 246, 539; O, 137, 160, 266.

[61]Farm Book.

[62]*Ibid.*, Dec. 31, 1852.

[63]*Ibid.*; Davis Papers. In 1855, Perry County had seventeen schools of the primary and secondary types attended by 1,036 pupils. Judson had 265 students; the Female Seminary, 120; and Howard, 70. Perry County, Unpublished Census Returns, 1855 (Office of Probate Court, Marion).

sociated with the Female Seminary as one of the founders and because he was a Methodist rather than Baptist. While living in Marion Davis was a regular attendant of the Methodist Church there and after moving to his plantation he attended services almost every Sunday at a Methodist Church in the little town of Hamburg, near which Beaver Bend was located. Whenever a protracted meeting was held either in Marion or Hamburg, he was usually present every night.[64]

Davis showed some interest, too, in the wide-spread temperance movement that became so pronounced in Alabama in the fifties. While he was a lawyer he drank whiskeys and wines, although not to excess, and he continued to drink moderately after he turned to planting.[65] On one occasion in 1855, however, following his attendance of a temperance lecture at the Hamburg Church, he wrote in his farm book that he had "engaged teetotalism for 12 months although I humbly trust precedent obligations [possibly to his wife who was a very devout Methodist] will carry me through life."[66] For some reason this period happened to be one in which he also demonstrated more interest than usual in religion, for within a week of the above "engagement" he purchased six Bibles and a New Testament.[67] What he did with them is unknown, although it is possible some of them were distributed among his slaves. Be that as it may, his promise to refrain from drink did not seem to bring him happiness and on November 22, 1856, on the occasion of his forty-fifth birthday, he made the following interesting entry in his farm book: "It was celebrated as usual, by a dinner, a gobbler—a pig & lamb—There was too much of the feast & not enough of the flow, too much flesh—too little Spirit. I am growing old rather more visibly than I am getting wiser."[68]

Davis was always interested in books and other publications. As early as 1838 he was subscribing to several almanacs, and in the next year he became a follower of the *American Phrenological Journal and Miscellany* (later known as the *Phrenological Journal and Science of Health*). Before 1848, his newspaper subscription list included *The Monitor, Southern Advocate, Marion Herald, Independent Monitor,* and the (Montgomery) *Alabama Journal.* He was more pleased,

[64]Davis Papers.
[65]Receipts, dated April, June, 1837; Jan. 23, 1841; Feb. 18, 1845, in Davis Papers.
[66]Farm Book, Apr. 15, 1855.
[67]*Ibid.,* Apr. 23, 1855.
[68]*Ibid.*

however, with *The Louisville* (Kentucky) *Journal* than any other newspaper, and subscribed to it most consistently.[69] Dozens of law books
were purchased annually until 1853, these and other works being obtained through a Tuscaloosa book dealer named D. Woodruff. He
bought a set of James Madison's *Papers* on one occasion and at another
time paid thirty dollars for Jared Sparks, *Life and Writings of Franklin*. He was familiar with French and secured a few books in that
language.[70]

Other reading interests were indicated when Woodruff sent Davis
the following list of books: "Liebey's Letters, Headley's Napoleon,
Headley's Washington, Thier's French Revolution, Prescott's Conquest,
Hallam's Constitutional History, [Samuel] Johnson's Lectures,
Brougham's Men of Letters, [and] Washington and His Generals."[71]
Another favorite was Alexander Pope's *Essay on Man,* particularly the
passage:

> Order is Heavens first law and this confessed
> Some are, and must be greater than the rest,
> More rich than wise; but who infers from hence
> That such are happier shock all common sense.

Another verse, perhaps his own, which appealed to Davis was,

> Come gentle Ceres, night & morn
> Inspire our Song, We write of Corn
> We Sing of rice, of Sweet potatoes
> And things to cheer our human natures.[72]

His plantation home at Beaver Bend contained a large room set aside
as a library, and it was always a popular place among the members of
the Davis family. Davis by the time of his death had collected a
personal library of 631 volumes.[73] Some of his books are still available
for examination and many of them contain numerous marginal notes
showing that he both read and enjoyed them.

In other respects, too, Davis followed the pattern of life set for
members of his class. He was a Mason and a member of at least one
other fraternal Order.[74] Although by no means did all planters of his
area live in mansions such as those sometimes pictured by popular

[69]Receipts, in Davis Papers. It has been impossible to decide upon the places of
publication of some of these newspapers.
[70]Farm Book, Mar. 24, 1859.
[71]Receipts, in Davis Papers.
[72]Farm Book, Dec. 31, 1853; *ibid.,* no date.
[73]Perry County, Inventory of Estates (Office of Probate Court, Marion), I, 928-935.
[74]Memorandum, dated 1843, in Davis Papers.

imagination, Davis was able to build a comfortable, quite elaborate home for his family at Beaver Bend. The grounds of the place were landscaped and planted with flowers, shrubbery, hedges, and trees. In one month alone, January, 1853, he had 750 yards of roses planted along a road fronting his plantation.[75]

The owner of Beaver Bend frequently made hunting and fishing trips, and on these excursions was often accompanied by his children. And in keeping with the old practice of teaching the son to work as well as the servant in order that the son might learn to earn his bread before eating it, the young people of the Davis family were often put to work. Sometimes they plowed the fields; at other times they rode about the plantation with their father.[76] The elder Davis and the family were always eager to attend one of the many barbecues or picnics arranged by acquaintances, and such affairs were often held at Beaver Bend, seemingly on the slightest excuse. Whenever any member of the family had a birthday the occasion was celebrated with a party. Davis himself was usually honored on his own birthday with a dinner, sometimes as many as six or seven neighboring families sitting down at the table to join in the festivities.[77] Also, as recorded by Davis on March 25, 1854, two families "& my own family dined out on the river Bank, this being [his son] Hugh's birthday."[78] All in all, the pleasures of the family were derived from unsophisticated pastimes and here, too, Davis was not unlike his contemporaries.

As often as possible, he visited his friends and neighbors and his wife's parents and relatives in Perry and Dallas Counties. He never travelled extensively, although he did usually manage at least one trip a year to Mobile. Pleasure was always combined with business on the trips. After 1851 he exchanged visits several times with his parents in Mississippi. On one occasion he went to New Orleans and at another time to Memphis. As far as can be determined, except for a visit to Virginia in 1861, where he went for his health, these few journeys com-

[75]Farm Book, Jan. 17-31, 1853; Sept. 1, 1855; Dec. 16, 1857; Jan. 20, 1860. For an excellent description of the types of houses actually lived in by many Southern planters of the late ante-bellum period, see James C. Bonner, "Plantation Architecture of the Lower South on the Eve of the Civil War," *Journal of Southern History,* XI (August, 1945), 371-388.

[76]Farm Book, Mar. 24, 1856.

[77]*Ibid.,* Nov. 22, 1853, 1857, and 1858, contain descriptions of celebrations of Davis birthdays.

[78]*Ibid.*

prised his travels. On the other hand, he frequently visited his neighbors in order to pay a call or to examine their crops and to compare the latter with his own. These visits were one of his simplest, nonetheless most enjoyable, pleasures, and on his return to Beaver Bend he always recorded his impressions of his friends' crops. On August 26, 1850, as he put it, he went to Dallas County and "Examined Messrs. Goree, Tubbs, W. A. & T. D. Jones Crops—all fine. Goree's superfine." On August 4, 1854, following a visit to Dallas County, he wrote in his farm book, "Thad's [T. D. Jones] crop is the very best crop of Cotton I ever Saw, better than ever I expected to See to the height of the Stalk —& it is high enough. The limbs begin near the ground and are long & Spreading, close together & crowded with bolls & Squares to tips & tops, & I believe that a Single Limb selected from each Stalk in his field will exceed in production one half the crops in Perry County." The next day, after a similar trip, he wrote that "The Dallas crops are very good—the corn especially—the cotton is large—& tolerably loaded —the rains have caused a loss by Shedding of the Squares—Mr. T. D. Jones is Still ahead of all the farmers I have Seen."[79]

Another pleasure presumably enjoyed by Davis was that of discussing with his friends the questions of slavery and politics. A planter living at the time and in the state where he resided could not have escaped such discussions even if he had so desired. But Davis' extensive correspondence and papers contain not a single significant reference to the slavery issue or Abolition Crusade which were raging at precisely the time he was managing his plantation. Even so, on occasion he must have been just as interested in the discussion of the slavery problem and its political aspects as he was in talking about the weather and his crops. One was as important to him as the other. But he wrote interminably about the weather, complaining when it was too hot, when it was too cold, when it rained too much, when it rained too little, and in general seemingly was never satisfied. His complaints became so strong on this score at times that it is really surprising that he continued to operate his plantation.[80] On the other hand, he wrote very little about politics or slavery, although this can perhaps be explained. His every-day interests, similar to those of most planters, were of a local nature, and condition of weather was all important to the farmer or

[79]*Ibid.; ibid.*, July 21, 1855.
[80]*Ibid., passim.*

planter.   Be that as it may, if he showed any great interest in politics there are no records available to prove it.   The only fact established concerning his political activity is that during the 1840's he consistently voted the Whig ticket and that, along with many other planters of the South,[81] he finally switched his support to the Democratic Party in 1856.[82]   His one reference of any importance in his farm book to the great political controversies of his time was made after the presidential election of the latter year, when he wrote, "the elemental Strife as well as the Political is hushed.   The nation reposes after months of excitement."[83]

As has already been stated, Davis began operating Beaver Bend in January, 1848, and for four years hesitated to abandon his lucrative law practice and give all of his attention to his plantation. Perhaps the reason for his hesitancy was the low price being received for cotton. In November, 1848, when his first crop was up for sale, some shipments of the staple to Mobile were bringing less than five cents a pound.[84]   Prices rose gradually for the next few years, however, and at a time when the price had almost doubled Davis moved out to his plantation.   In September, 1851, about three months before he began his residence at Beaver Bend, a glowing account of prosperity in Mobile was circulated. It was that

The number of buildings completed is greater than in any preceding year; and still so great is the demand for them, rents are advancing. Public buildings are now under contract in the city, the estimated cost of which is over half a million dollars. Nine new steamboats are also building for the Mobile trade the coming year. Much of this city activity is doubtless owing to the increase in the receipts of cotton at this port of over 100,000 bales [in 1851 over 1850], and to the uninterrupted health which has uniformly prevailed.[85]

Between 1848 and December, 1851, when Davis assumed personal management of his plantation, there were many other evidences of a growing prosperity both in Perry County and through the Alabama blackbelt.   Of local importance was the construction of many new bridges and roads and the fact that the Cahaba and Marion Railroad

[81]For Southern support of the Whig Party, see Arthur Charles Cole, *The Whig Party in the South* (Washington, 1913), *passim.*
[82]Farm Book, Aug. 3, 1857, contains: "This day being election day I went to Hamburg & voted the Democratic ticket, the first except the presidential vote last fall."
[83]*Ibid.,* Nov. 5, 1856.
[84]J. R. Goree to Davis, Nov. 24, 1848, in Davis Papers.   Goree was a commission merchant in Mobile.
[85]*Mobile Journal of Commerce Letter-Sheet Price-Current,* Sept. 1, 1851, in Jones Papers.

was nearing completion.[86] Cahaba, the Alabama River port for many of the Perry County planters, was booming,[87] as were other towns along the river.[88] By 1850, Perry County had taken its place with others in the blackbelt as one of the seven largest cotton producing counties in the state.[89] Negro labor was ample, and as early as 1840 the slaves in the county had outnumbered the whites. The state itself, with its rich blackbelt soil and excellent climate, produced 564,429 bales of cotton in 1850, and had established itself as the leading cotton producing state in the country. Perry County, with a population of 9,425 whites, of which 1,081 owned slaves in 1850, had its share in acquiring such a reputation for the state. A total of 419 persons owned more than ten slaves.[90] More cotton was produced between 1850 and 1860 than in any ten year period before the Civil War. The increase in the number of slave owners in Perry County shows that it went along with the rest of the South in a rush to produce more and more cotton. In 1855, the population of the county had increased to 22,782, with 14,661 of this total being slaves. Of 1,861 white males over twenty-one years of age, 457 now owned more than ten slaves, in comparison with 419 in that class in 1850. Sixty-three whites owned between 50 and 100 slaves; ten owned between 100 and 200; and the largest planter, whose name was L. Q. C. DeYampert, the only one having more than 200, owned 245 Negroes. Altogether there were 913 slave owners in the county. In 1860, there were 9,479 whites and 18,245 blacks in the county.[91]

Davis was quite correct in 1851 in believing that it was an opportune time to begin his career as an active planter. He resided at Beaver Bend until July, 1861, when, because of ill health, he moved back to his town home in Marion. He died on June 6, 1862.[92] During his life

[86]Perry County, Minutes, Commissioners Court, A, 184-186, 304, 305, 310. In 1851, a very elaborate system of delivery of the mails was established in Perry County. E. H. Bernhard to Davis, May 6, 1851, in Davis Papers.

[87]See Anna M. Gayle Fry, *op. cit.,* 17-18, 25-26.

[88]For an account of the importance of Montgomery, Alabama, to 1846, see Clanton W. Williams, "Early Ante-Bellum Montgomery: A Black-Belt Constituency," *Journal of Southern History,* VII (November, 1941), 495-525.

[89]The other blackbelt counties were: Dallas, Greene, Lowndes, Marengo, Montgomery, and Wilcox. Davis, *The Cotton Kingdom in Alabama,* p. 199.

[90]*Ibid.,* pp. 40, 42, 194-196.

[91]Perry County, Unpublished Census Returns, 1855; Owen, *op. cit.,* p. 110.

[92]*Marion Commonwealth,* June 7, 1862. On June 1, 1859, Davis had a paralytic stroke. After his attack he could barely move, and in 1860 he recorded that he had been to "Hot Springs, Va., White Sulphur Healing Springs, Bath Alum, Warms & also Richmond. . . . Still I am Strictly an invalid." Farm Book, Nov. 22, 1860. See *ibid.,* July 8-13, 1861, for information on his return to Marion.

in Alabama he helped in a small way in transforming the state from an Indian country into one of the outstanding agricultural, commercial and cultural regions in the South.[93] In no sense, however, did he ever attract any state-wide attention as a planter, nor was he even the largest land- and slave-owner or successful farmer in Perry County. He never made any startling discoveries in methods of farming; neither did he ever produce enormous amounts of cotton. In most respects, he was merely an average Alabama blackbelt planter of the 1850's, going about his own business, although he did own more acres of land and more slaves than the average planter of his county. Yet his activities merit close attention for the simple reason that some personalities are important without being leaders. If plantation life is to be understood more fully, it is necessary to inquire more minutely into the lives of individual planters and into everyday aspects of life on their plantations. Both Davis and Beaver Bend are worthy examples of inquiry. How the plantation was managed by the Davis family will be told in some detail in subsequent chapters of this study. Now that the general setting of Davis' mature life has been described, it is proper to turn to a discussion of his specific methods of operating Beaver Bend, as well as to other phases of activities there, and then to carry the story through the periods of the Civil War and afterwards.

[93]See Minnie Claire Boyd, *Alabama in the Fifties; A Social Study* (New York, 1931), *passim.*

2

PLANTATION MANAGEMENT: SCIENTIFIC FARMING

I N THE LIGHT of present-day agricultural knowledge it is perhaps unjustified to state that Hugh Davis was a scientific farmer.[1] Still, it seems unwise to pass judgment either on him or on his contemporaries solely on grounds of modern criteria. It is true that Alabama blackbelt planters of the ante-bellum period in most cases failed to practice rotation of crops or diversification. But at the same time it should be remembered that they reached Alabama at a period when cotton was becoming the great money crop of the Deep South. Because it was the established custom to plant cotton they planted it. The practice was widely followed in Alabama long before Davis became a farmer. Moreover, many of the state's planters, from their arrival, failed to protect the fertility of the land which they controlled, this being the case for two possible reasons. There was the overpowering profit motive in the continuous production of cotton, as well as the seemingly inexhaustible supply of rich, virgin lands. If land could not have been obtained in Alabama, they could have gone elsewhere. As a

[1]The study from this point is for the most part an expression of the writer's interpretations and conclusions based on a long study of farm books or diaries kept by Hugh Davis, his overseers, and his sons. Unless otherwise stated, the source for the information in the present and succeeding chapters is the farm books. All letters referred to, unless otherwise explained, are to be found in the Davis Papers. Other materials will be referred to in the usual manner.

result, relatively few planters bothered to pamper land, for the simple reason that it was plentiful and could be bought on ridiculously easy terms. Even so, some of them did make conscientious, persistent efforts to operate their establishments in a manner which they considered to be systematic and scientific. With certain qualifications, Davis was a member of this group. He consistently sought means of improving the soil at Beaver Bend, worked out rules of procedure and enforced them, kept a detailed check on operations, and usually demonstrated great initiative and resourcefulness in the management of his plantation. For these reasons, if for no others, he must be considered as a scientific farmer, although by no means in the modern sense.

During his lifetime and afterwards Davis was considered by his friends to have been an excellent farmer and, according to tradition, he was one of the most successful planters in Perry County in the decade before the Civil War. His information on the methods of farming that he generally followed came in the usual ways. He was a member of a planter family and lived in an agricultural region all his life. Some advice on farming in the Alabama blackbelt no doubt came to him from the members of his wife's family, for several of them were quite successful planters both in Perry and Dallas Counties. Probably of most importance in his case, however, as well as in that of many of his contemporaries, was the information on farming which he gained from reading numerous ante-bellum newspapers and other publications available to the people living in and near the Alabama blackbelt. Like most planters of his period, Davis subscribed to several newspapers, farm journals and other periodicals which specialized in accounts on farm methods. Too, he often followed advices contained in the numerous almanacs which were distributed so freely in his region. In 1847, after he had decided to become a planter, he began buying farm books and manuals to be studied in his new work. One such group of works, bought in 1847, consisted of "Agricultural History, Farmer's Dictionary, Agricultural Arts, Agricultural Catechism, Poultry Book, [and] Ladies Garderner."[2]

After 1848, because of his new interests and activities, his subscription list of newspapers naturally assumed a more pronounced agricultural character; and among the publications to which he subscribed most regularly after 1848, as he designated them, were *The Ledger*,

[2]D. Woodruff to Davis, July 3, 1847, in Davis Papers.

The Southern Cultivator, The Cotton Planter, The Louisville Journal, and the *Daily* (Montgomery) *Alabama Journal.* Worthy of special note is the list of newspapers he took in 1858. Included were *The Washington Union, Montgomery Advertiser, Marion Commonwealth, Marion American Weekly, The Southern Cultivator, The Cotton Planter & Soil,* and the *New York Day Book.*³ Of the publications, Davis' favorite was *The Southern Cultivator* and he read it at least from 1853 to 1859. It was also quite popular among his friends and neighbors in the vicinity of Beaver Bend, as witnessed by his organization in 1853, in cooperation with nine other planters, of what he termed the "Club for the Cultivator." After the first year only five of the original group continued as active members of the "Club." Included were two of Davis' brothers-in-law, O. T. and R. T. Jones. The arrangement was to divide the cost of subscription, and after the *Cultivator* was received at Beaver Bend and read by Davis it was circulated among the members. By reading this publication and the many to which they subscribed, Davis and his colleagues became acquainted with what were considered the best available farming practices of their day. Between 1839 and 1859, he subscribed to more than twenty different newspapers and periodicals. Many of his practices at Beaver Bend of course resulted from information obtained by reading these publications.

On the other hand, Davis possessed many weaknesses as a scientific farmer. After obtaining new information on the most approved methods of farming he often reverted to old, customary, time-worn practices.⁴ In fact, he sometimes went about his management of Beaver Bend in a fashion against which he had been specifically warned. For example, although he seemed to have developed an interest in labor-saving machinery he always depended on manual labor. In April, 1849, he bought a corn sheller, but afterwards never referred to its use. Rather the work was done by hand by his slaves. In 1852, he borrowed a wheat thresher from a neighbor; but after using it recorded that it was not satisfactory. Afterwards, this work was also done by hand.⁵

³It has been impossible to determine the precise titles or places and dates of publication of all of these newspapers. It should be mentioned, however, that *The Southern Cultivator* was begun in 1843 in Athens, Georgia. Today it is printed in Atlanta, and is still a well known publication.
⁴*Farm Book, passim.*
⁵*Ibid.,* Aug. 16, 1852; *ibid., passim.*

The only conclusion to be reached about Davis as a scientific farmer is that he was a paradox. In some respects, as will be shown, he was advanced for his period. In other respects, he seemingly refused to take advantage of practices which might have improved the operation of his plantation. It seems also that he might have at least attended some of the agricultural fairs and exhibits which were held so frequently in Alabama in the 1850's. But he was present at only one such affair, and then almost nine years after he became a planter. His reactions, recorded in his farm book on November 14, 1856, were as follows: "Returned from Montgomery: fatigued & Compensated for the 30$ in money Spent—it being my first visit to any agricultural Show. My views may be thus written. 1st Class animals, Single women—2 widows —3 widowers—4th Jackasses. 5th Devon Bulls. Lastly Dunhams & Berkshires—1 Class machines—Wheat Thresher—Wheat fan—Cast iron mill. The crowd on the 3rd day was immense."

A special feature of Davis' management of Beaver Bend was the emphasis which he put on various lists of rules of procedure which he worked out and wrote intermittently in his farm books. To write down such rules was not at all uncommon, but Davis' are significant because of their completeness as well as his consistent adherence to them in his everyday operations. Indeed, the first entry which he made in his first farm book was a brief list of directions designated by him as "GENERAL RULES & DIRECTIONS EVERY YEAR." Eight different aspects of plantation management were mentioned, although all of them had to do with general operations. These rules are of special importance here because they represent Davis' original ideas on certain phases of farm activities, and also because they were never repealed from the date of their inception, January, 1848, until their orginator's death in June, 1862. Davis' many references to them show that they became a permanent part of the general order of procedure at Beaver Bend. Under the date of January 1, 1848, they are to be found in his farm book:

Let the plows Start the 15th January; Begin to plant corn 15th February; Begin to plant cotton 15th March; Keep Stock *in* the lots & *out* of the fields; Buy neith[er] meat nor bread; See that everything keeps its proper place; Who is that faithful & wise Steward, whom his employer Shall make ruler over his Household, to give them their portion in due Season? He, Whom, his employer, when he cometh Shall find him So doing. Luke XII, 42 & 43. But if the Steward Shall Say in his heart, my *Employer* delayed his coming & Shall begin to beat the men-servants & the maidens & to eat &

drink & *to be drunken,* the Employer will come in a day when he looketh not for him, & will cut in sunder the contract & Say: thou mayest no longer be Steward here; and those Servants which know the Stewards well and the master's rules and do not according thereto, shall be beaten with many Stripes. But he that knew them not Shall receive very few Stripes.

In addition to the above general rules Davis drew up at the same time a more detailed group of "Special rules to the Overseer." Twelve points were mentioned, most of them relating to the overseer's relations and duties in connection with the Beaver Bend slaves. For that reason those particular points are discussed at a later, more appropriate place in this study. Included in the rules for the overseer, however, were two items of a general nature, and they are worthy of notice here. One stated that no fences were to be taken down or left down, nor were any fences to be left lying on the ground if they accidently fell out of place. The other rule required that all mending and repairing of damaged plantation equipment should be done at the earliest time convenient. Davis thus began operations at Beaver Bend with certain general procedures in mind.

From 1848 onward Davis gradually evolved more and more elaborate directions for the management of his plantation. Finally, on June 1, 1862, less than a week before his death, he established a detailed set of orders in which he included nearly every rule which he had previously originated. These, his last rules, represent the results of his experiences as a planter and despite the fact that they were decreed after the beginning of the Civil War they are included here as a part of Davis' operations before 1861 because such detailed instruction could have resulted only from long experience and practice. Moreover, an examination of the various Davis farm books before 1862 has shown that most of the general methods, as described in 1862, had been in use long before the description itself was recorded. The directions were designated by Davis as his "System of farming at Beaver Bend, Its Principles, Its Rules and Its Regulations."[6] He stated first that the principles of the "System" concerned only himself because he was the owner, that the rules were to be followed by himself and his overseer, and that the regulations were for the benefit of everyone, including the

[6]See Weymouth T. Jordan (ed.), " 'System of Farming at Beaver Bend,' Alabama, 1862," *Journal of Southern History,* VII (February, 1941), 76-84, for an edited version of the "System" as recorded by Davis in his farm book. See also the same editor's "The Management Rules of an Alabama Black Belt Plantation, 1848-1862," *Agricultural History,* XVIII (January, 1944), 53-64.

slaves, who lived at Beaver Bend. He declared that "The 'principle' is that the plantation must be governed by a code of love suited to the patriarchal rather than the civil." He, "first in rank," was to lay down the principles, the rules and the regulations; the overseer was to follow all rules and enforce them as well as the regulations; and the slaves were to work "well under the overseer."

Davis asserted that the first objective was to "buy neither bread nor meat nor anything that can be made on the place," and articles mentioned specifically as those being made were: plow stocks, ax handles, hoe helves, harness, horse collars, leading lines, and well ropes. All materials, except iron, needed in the plantation shop and blacksmith shop were obtained at home. Manure was saved from the horse lot, the cow pens, the sheep pound and the hog pens, to be used in fertilizing corn, cotton, small grain, garden vegetables, and other farm produce. One acre of corn was planted each year to furnish fodder for each horse and mule on the place. Peas were also planted to supply feed for the animals. Corn acreage each year amounted to at least half the combined acreage of cotton and oats. Vegetables were to be planted "in sufficient quantities to supply the hands three times every day," and half an acre planted in wheat and three acres for garden plots were set aside for the use of the Negroes. As a cotton crop, Davis planned to plant twelve acres each year to be cultivated by each slave, and he expected to make "every good season an 500 lbs. bale to every one acre and a half planted. . . ." The stock was kept under fence, pastured during the day, and fed with cotton seed and hay at night. Plowing before seed were planted was done as deeply as the strength of the teams would allow, but after the seed were in the ground it was ordered that plowing be done as lightly as possible, "perhaps the first plowing of corn excepted." Negro hands were pushed fast at their work during the planting season, that is, until late in the spring, after which time they were given two hours free from field labor at noon each day. The hog feeder and stock feeder counted the animals in their charge, and were directed to give them proper feed. Davis' final advice was: "In all matters not specifically provided for, sound reason and common sense may be called in as guides, but the practice on other plantations will only lead astray where these guides are rejected." These were the general rules of 1862. Rules for the overseers and the slaves will be discussed later.

One other requirement included in the "System" is worthy of particular notice here, however. It was that the overseer should read every three months the rules and regulations which had been established, and that "a daily record shall be made in short stating the things most worthy to be recorded—how much well or ill done, all increase, all loss with causes and manner, the quantities harvested, the prices sold for and the interest on capital, as near as may be the contents of the place in acres, and by whom measured, and the production as compared with former years." In keeping with this requirement, Davis had started at the very beginning of his planter career to keep a written record of events at Beaver Bend. But unfortunately for the historian, the entire record was not as complete as Davis required in his 1862 rules. If the requirement had been executed properly the story of Beaver Bend would be almost complete. Altogether there are six farm books extant, however, and from them especially has come this study. The character of the records is shown by the following random examples taken from the first farm book. On May 3, 1850, Davis wrote: "Examined crop, corn cotton etc. The corn is improving, but is not looking good. Cotton is crisped as if a blast of fire had rapidly passed over it. The Stand is below ordinary, or average, but with pains or care in cultivating will be sufficient. . . . The plowing in Some places is difficult owing to baking rains. The mules are galled & the collars want mending."

An entry made shortly afterwards in the farm book, on June 9, 1850, was:

The lice have very nearly all left the cotton. . . . The places where the stand is hurt are . . . in those places the soil is quite exhausted & poor. The general Stand is Superior to last years & the lice eaten Spots smaller. . . .

The corn grows Slowly, rather below expectations—is now and then Showing a tassle in a manured Spot, but is low & small in these places . . .

Wheat. This was cut the 5th June, injured a good deal by rust, and yielding a poor return—it was sowed in Dec.

Oats. These . . . are quite Small and low. The land is Sandy & thin & the yield well light. . . .

Teams are improving in appearance but are thin.

Hoggs are in the woods—they look tolerably well but need corn.

Garden. Here has been considerable improvement, and yet a good deal may be done. Rain is wanted—& so is a little work.

General Improvements. A new wagon Shelter & well House are now to be seen— both have been long wanted.

This matter of keeping a record of affairs at Beaver Bend was dear to Davis, and he always insisted that it be done. It was the one requirement of his overseers which he emphasized most consistently. As will be shown later several overseers were discharged because they failed to carry out Davis' wishes in this respect. On his part, Davis considered that maintenance of the record was absolutely necessary for the successful management and operation of his plantation. It is only because of the negligence of some of his overseers that the record is incomplete.

In keeping with his general plan of operation, and following a custom widely practiced by planters, Davis had his Negroes clear some new land for cultivation each year at Beaver Bend. The method employed in opening up new land for use was always the same. Trees were felled; some were split into rails for use in constructing fences; others were sent to nearby mills where they were dressed off as lumber; some of the logs were used in constructing Negro cabins; and those not used were rolled into large piles or heaps and burned. After the trees were removed, the slaves then collected and burned the underbrush. Next, the land was broken up with plows, and finally prepared for the crop which was to be planted. Ordinarily no attempt was made to remove tree stumps during the first few years a new piece of land was under cultivation. The job of clearing and preparing land was usually one of the chief tasks of the slaves during the months of January and February. During these months, however, they also made general improvements, and knocked down cotton and corn stalks on old land, burned trash, made collars and baskets from corn shucks, spun cloth, made harness, dug ditches, made hoe handles, constructed or repaired gates, fences and Negro cabins, and shelled peas and corn. Usually the land newly cleared was planted in cotton during its first year of cultivation, although sometimes corn and peas instead were put in the new land. Davis seems not to have had any rule concerning this matter during his first years at Beaver Bend, but in the late fifties he always put new land in corn and peas. At no time, however, did Davis state that he realized the value of planting the legumes in new land. It merely seemed to improve his land and accordingly he followed the practice. Nor did he consistently indicate the amount of land which was cleared each year. Nevertheless, this matter may be partially clarified by mentioning the number of plows run each year. At least the figures show that there was a gradual increase in the amount of land under cultivation. Ten plows were in use in 1854, ten in 1855, fourteen in 1856, sixteen in 1857 and 1858, nineteen in 1859 and 1860, and twenty in 1861. It is known, too, that fifty-two acres of fresh land were planted in 1854, seventy-five acres in 1857, and at least three new fields, of undetermined sizes, in 1861.

From the amount of logs which were burned each year while land was being cleared, it seems that Beaver Bend was amply supplied with an excellent stand of timber. On one occasion, February 18, 1859, an overseer recorded that 430 piles or heaps of logs had been burned from only twenty-five acres of new land, "the most I ever saw." A year later a smaller field resulted in at least 194 piles. Although an enormous amount of timber must have been wantonly wasted each year in this manner, a great quantity was also employed in the construction of fences around the new lands as they were cleared. Davis' interests in fences is mentioned in the following observation made on February 29, 1856, in his farm book, eight years after he began his farming activities. The statement is taken from his summary of the work accomplished at the plantation during the month of February: ". . . in this month and Jany got about 15 thousand rails!!! This is a heavy outlay of labor & awful destructive of timber & I hope to cease from and after this year and do Some cleaning, after which I begin to plant on fair terms of Success; Since I began my planting operations I have cleared 180 acres of land, built about 30 houses of all kinds—made at least 50,000 rails, dug 7 miles of ditches — & therefore have never had a chance to compete with others in my cotton bales." Even if large amounts of timber were used in the construction of fences, houses, cabins, bridges, gates and structures of other kinds, an enormous quantity of wood was still destroyed. For the waste incurred Davis might be censured, but if that is necessary it should be remembered that he was merely following a very common practice when he destroyed timber. The practice has been prevalent among most agriculturists and others throughout the greater part of the history of the United States, the reason of course being the belief that the supply of timber was almost inexhaustible. Davis was a product of his times.

While clearing and fencing his lands and planting it in corn, cotton, peas and other crops, Davis also turned to another custom which was common among the planters of his region. He had his slaves haul load after load of stable manure to the various fields of the plantation, and literally covered some of his fields with the fertilizer. Other kinds of domestic fertilizer, especially cotton seed, were used on occasion, but in the main stable manure was the stand-by. In fact, the saving of manure was always one of the important duties intrusted to the Beaver Bend overseers, and special bins were constructed for storing the waste during those seasons of the year when it was not necessary to spread it. A customary task of the slaves during the winter months was to rake up manure from the various plantation stables and stock lots and to store it away in the bins. The job was also performed during rainy seasons when it was impossible to carry on the usual farm work because of inclement weather.

The first definite reference in a farm book to the use of manure was made in the spring of 1852, when it was recorded that both stable manure and cotton seed were being thrown out to fertilize land on which cotton and corn were being planted. In the fall of the same year, cotton seed was also scattered over land which was being prepared for sowing wheat. The next year Davis started piling up cotton seed to rot before being used as fertilizer. Greater quantities of manure were used as fertilizer in February, 1854, than ever before. Also in 1854, he put cattle in the plantation garden plots to manure them. Again, in 1857, a hog lot was plowed up and planted in cotton. In April, 1854, he turned to the use of what he termed a "homemade guano." Although no information is available concerning the method by which this guano was prepared, it was probably a mixture of stable manure and cotton seed with which experiments were made at this time. Be that as it may, the guano was spread over two acres of cotton land, and on April 8 the overseer was instructed to "See what improvement takes place in the cotton from this manure." On August 22, Davis himself reported on the results of the experiment. The first picking on the two acres amounted to 377 pounds of seed cotton, or 188½ pounds to the acre. The first picking of the thirty-acre Mathew Jones field, so-called, which had been fertilized with manure alone, and which was considered as the best piece of land on the plantation, amounted to 3,677 pounds, or only 122½ pounds to the acre. On this basis it might be supposed that Davis was satisfied with his home-made guano, but he failed to record the results of later pickings. Therefore it is impossible to ascertain either the final success of the experiment or his reactions to it.

In the years after his experiment with his domestic guano, Davis used a mixture of cotton seed and stable manure intermittently. Sometimes separately and at times together they were the chief fertilizers employed at Beaver Bend from 1854 until 1862. They were always utilized especially in preparing land for corn and cotton, and in successive years larger and larger amounts were scattered. Whether this was done because the land was wearing out is not known, but that possibility should at least be mentioned. In the spring of 1855, Davis figured that he was using one-half wagon load of cotton seed to each acre of corn. He also computed that 2,904 hills of corn were planted to each acre, and that thirty-six bushels of seed were spread on each acre. In addition he began planting the hills three feet apart and had his Negroes drop one handful of stable manure on each hill. Other crops besides corn were fertilized. Cotton of course received great attention. The method of planting Irish potatoes is of particular interest, being described on March 9, 1855, as follows: "Planted a part of my Irish potatoes in trenches made with the Spade 1 foot deep, filled partly with little chips & Stable manure & then the potatoes planted covered with Hog's hair & then with Common earth—Rows 3½ feet wide. The object is to manure the ground thoroughly as well as to make potatoes." Another mixture, used in 1856 to fertilize Irish potatoes, consisted of ashes, stable manure, and cotton seed. Once, pine tags, ashes and bone dust were spread over cotton land. On February 26, 1857, the Negroes "circled around the roots of Apple trees & hauled manure for the rings." In 1859, a fertilizer was made by mixing stable manure, leaf mould, and scrapings from newly cleared land. This mixture was used again in 1860. It was made by raking up dead leaves and putting them in cow and sheep pens. After the leaves and other scrapings which had been added remained in the pens for a few days, they were raked up again to be used as "maneur."

The only time Davis ever employed a commercial fertilizer was in 1859, and even then it was used in conjunction with cotton seed. In September, three bags of guano were purchased to be utilized in preparing five acres of wheat. On October 31, its use was described by the overseer: "We have sowed our wheat—the plan is this—we first broke the land with double plows then sowed 30 bushels of cotton Seed to the acre then sowed the wheat and ploughed it in with Scooters then Spread about 60 lbs. of guano to the acre then drug A heavy brush over it. . . ." How this experiment turned out is not known, but it seems that afterwards Davis still considered stable manure as the best fertilizer, and he continued to spread large quantities over various fields of the plantation until the close of the ante-bellum period. Cotton seed was also scattered. In 1860, ninety-eight wagon loads of manure were thrown out in the fields in one five day period. An undetermined, but large, number of wagon loads of seed were hauled to new ground when it was cleared in February, 1861. And, as had become the custom, the seed was first placed in cow pens to pick up manure before it was spread out. In one week in March, 1861, eighty-eight wagon loads of manure were hauled to the thirty-acre Mathew Jones field. Davis figured that each load contained seventy-two bushels of manure. Therefore, 6,336 bushels were scattered during the week. Even this amount, however, does not represent the total number of loads, because others were hauled to the field later in the month. The Mathew Jones field and another one known as the Mock Orange field were always most heavily manured and therefore produced more cotton than any other sections of the plantation. This is borne out by a statement, made on June 30, 1860, by an overseer who happened to be the son of a blackbelt planter, that "I think the Mock orange & M. Jones will Compare with any Cotton in the Neighbourhood or out of it either."

Besides clearing, fencing and manuring his land, Davis was of course faced with the problem of solving other particulars of plantation management. One was the matter of soil erosion, and the manner in which he attempted to handle the matter shows that he was an unusual planter. He had to experiment and naturally made some mistakes because of the general lack of knowledge on the subject. Even so, he began early in his career to make conscientious efforts to keep his land from washing. In the beginning he merely followed the time-worn customs of his day. In 1853, potato vines were used to fill gullies to prevent further washing. Pine needles were thrown in washes in several fields of the plantation in 1853 and 1854. But after gathering the pine needles used for the purpose mentioned, slaves cut down the nearby pine trees and this of course speeded up erosion in the fields thereafter. It should be remembered, however, that Davis and his colleagues did not have the advantage of our present-day knowledge of erosion prevention. On August 19, 1855, ditches were cut across several large fields "to prevent land from washing," and from this time onward Davis showed much interest in the construction of an extremely elaborate system of ditches throughout the low lands of his place.

Not only were the ditches employed for the purpose of drawing off water during rainy seasons, but strikingly enough they were also used to irrigate the lower portions of the plantation during dry seasons, water for irrigation purposes being brought in from the Cahaba River. What was termed as "the long ditch" was dug partially across Beaver Bend, and opened into the river. As early as March 9, 1854, after a heavy rain, Davis recorded that his slaves were "opening the Sluices or inlets to dry the lands near the ditches." The opening seems to have worked too well, for during the following week the slaves were busy at the job of deepening the ditches in order to get water back up from the river. Then, a short time later, when another heavy downpour came the ditches were once more opened in order to allow excess water to drain off. In the next year Davis attempted a rather interesting experiment in his efforts to hit upon a better system of controlling water. Besides continuing to dig ditches in one plantation field, his Negroes, on March 10, 1855, "dug 3 pits 4 feet wide 3 feet deep . . ., the object being to dry wet places by drainage and evaporation." No report was made of the success of this experiment, and as is so often the case it is unknown how this one turned out. At no later time, moreover, is any reference made in the Davis farm books to the construction of other such pits. In all probability they were unsuccessful in their purpose.

Because of the location of Beaver Bend, with the Cahaba River as the plantation's crescent, Davis owned a large amount of river bottom land. And, similar to most planters and farmers he recognized that land located along the river bank was possibly the best on which to plant corn. Unfortunately for Davis, whenever the river overflowed it not only inundated much of his corn land, but often flooded it so completely that it threatened to ruin his entire corn crop. His solution of this problem, at least in one instance, was to construct a levee along the bank of the river at the point where it usually overflowed. As he put it, on February 21, 1855, the levee was built "to Stay the waters that overflow my new ground." No elaborate levee system was constructed at this time or later, however, but instead Davis continued with his ditching which could be used for two purposes, that is, for irrigation and drainage. As a matter of fact, after 1854 his low lands were ditched in such a way that they could be irrigated partially. In May, 1855, water was several times turned into the low lands on which corn had been planted. Two Negro slaves who performed the job of ditching were kept busy at their task. On May 21, their progress was recorded as follows by Davis: "I am irrigating the lowlands & improving the State of things, but the new ground is wanting it faster than it gets." A possible reason for this failure to get water to the new ground was the method then being followed in constructing ditches. Shallow ditches had been dug as new ground had been cleared each year, and as the necessity for more water arose the ditches had been deepened. Moreover, the whole system of ditches, as planned, had not yet been completed. By February, 1856, however, seven miles of ditches had been dug by Davis' hands during the eight years since he moved to Beaver Bend.

In the summer of 1856, a plan of irrigation also had been worked out by which it was hoped that water could be obtained for use in nearly all of the low land on the plantation. A ditch known as the "line cut" was completed, running across the entire place. Connected with it was a very elaborate system of ditches opening into the river. They were still not of much use in time of heavy rains, however, for on June 10 Davis fussed, "This morning—The world is nearly under water—last nights rain Surpassed any thing we have ever had in the way of rain— Everything is flooded—no ditches, rows,—embankments or contrivances availed." A little while later he turned back to his original idea on the ditches, that of using them for irrigation purposes. On July 28 they were tested, Davis stating, "Stopped my ditches & I began to irrigate my crop in the bottom, it is hardly called for, but I wish to see in case rain is delayed many more days whether the line cut and road cut, can be reached by my present plan." The ditches must have served their purpose, for following 1856 Davis stated time after time in his farm books that he irrigated parts of his land. There is no way of determining just how much was irrigated, however. In 1857, he began to cultivate rice; and it is known that in the last few years of the ante-bellum period he was able to irrigate a large portion of his low lands. To do so was indeed unusual for a planter of his region. It was possible, however, only because Beaver Bend was largely surrounded by the Cahaba River. But to say the least, the setting up of an irrigation system and the desire and necessary initiative to undertake such a task marks Davis as a scientific farmer.

His methods of plowing and planting certain of his crops were also conducted in the most approved manner. A few instances will suffice to bear out this point. In 1854, about an acre of clover was planted with two drills to the bed and then covered with a board. Sometime later one of the plantation overseers stated that corn was planted "with three double plows—run two furrows then rared it up with hoes making considerable ridge on the corn—A new plan to me." Six days later the overseer added that in planting the corn he had "1st Open[ed] with a Shovel full. 2 Then dropped 4 or 5 grs of corn 2½ feet, then run four furrows & followed with hoes Covering, breaking Clods, etc." The usual method of breaking clods with hoes did not suit Davis and in 1858 he hit upon a new system. To break up clods he had his slaves roll heavy logs over the ground which had been clodded. This system was continued and the next year, on May 2, 1859, an overseer wrote, "We have now in operation A clod breaker which give satisfaction to the esquire—it is decidedly worth running." On the other hand, in the spring of 1860 a later overseer stated that he had tried "Mr. D's plan of breaking Clods by rolling a large log over it but it had no effect on them and now I await and pray for a rain." But to return to the subject. In 1860, Irish potato rows were ploughed three feet apart; and corn five feet apart with a distance of two and one-half feet between each hill, and two grains of corn were placed in each hill. The express purpose of all this was to plant these crops in such a way that each separate plant could grow without crowding, as well as benefit to the utmost from the soil. As already mentioned, Davis also always insisted that in preparing land for crops the furrows be plowed as deeply as possible. He kept a close check on his ploughmen and considered their work to be among the most important tasks performed at Beaver Bend.

Another indication of Davis' scientific bent was his efforts to protect his crops from the ravages of worms, lice, birds, and other pests. Unfortunately for him, a great pestilence for cotton growers appeared in Alabama at the very time he began his operations. It was a pest known as the cotton worm. The worms turned up at Beaver Bend during Davis' first year there, and were present intermittently throughout his career as a planter. In July and August, 1848, Davis wrote repeatedly in his farm book of the havoc the worms were causing to his cotton. They became so bad about August 10 that the cotton squares were nearly all destroyed and the blooming of the cotton almost ceased. Davis was of the opinion that the worm was "not so numerous as it is voracious. One worm is fully capable of destroying one dozen well filled Stalks." Although he was discouraged at the outlook, he immediately made an effort to get rid of the pests. Six slaves were put in one of the cotton fields to see if they could destroy the worms there. They pulled off the worms and killed them, but after a week of this Davis dejectedly concluded that the experiment had "proved of no advantage," despite the killing of thousands of worms. Conditions became still worse when another pest, known locally as the army worm, put in its appearance. For Davis the result was the ruination of much of his 1848 cotton crop. Again in 1849 another scourge became evident. This time it was a pest designated as lice. On June 22, 1849, he complained that "The lice were this Season much worse on the tops and sides of ridges than in the bottoms and low places. This was the case generally as I learn from others as well as from those I have Seen." Even if he was unable to do anything at this time to check the worms and the lice, he at least observed where they were most numerous.

In 1850, he tried another method of getting rid of worms. He had his overseer direct the Negroes to lay full length beach trees, bodies and laps cut, on cotton lands for a period of one day. Because of the generally accepted belief that the odor of beach trees would cause insects to disperse,[7] Davis confidently stated, May 19, that this practice would

[7]For contemporary descriptions of this practice and many others of a somewhat similar nature in ante-bellum Alabama, see Weymouth T. Jordan (ed.), "Martin Mar-

"pay 500 per cent." But such was not the case, and it was noticed soon that lice were still numerous on the cotton, especially on land which had been planted in cotton the previous year, as well as in those fields which were thinnest and highest. It was observed too, that manured spots did not seem to be injured at all and that the lice put in their appearance particularly after rainy weather. Thus Davis continued to learn something of the habits of lice and worms, although he was still unable to develop any preventive which was successful.

On July 5, 1850, still another type of cotton worm turned up at Beaver Bend. This time, after examining them, Davis stated that they were not the usual kind of bore worm, but a "Smooth velvet brown, marked with a white line on each side." In his attempts to kill off these new pests, he borrowed two ideas from blackbelt friends of his. One method was called topping, in which the heads and tops of cotton branches were cut off and carried away from the cotton fields. It was supposed that a fly was responsible for the worms and that it laid its eggs in the top branches of cotton plants, and that by removing the top branches the worms would be prevented in the future. The practice was borrowed from a neighbor in Perry County. The other method employed in killing worms came to Davis from a planter living in Greene County, and after using it Davis concluded it to be the most effective way of destroying them. A mixture of molasses and vinegar was placed on a plate, and one plate was put at some point in each acre of cotton. After eating from the mixture the worms died by the thousands.

As was so often the case, however, it seems that Beaver Bend finally had to rely on nature to solve the difficult task of eradicating pests. On August 9, 1850, its owner reported that the weather was "hot & dry beyond anything I remember to have ever Seen. . . . Sunshine is the life of Cotton WORMS. Very few can be found, and they are confined to the Hogue field." Whether it was the hot weather, the mixture of molasses and vinegar mentioned above, or some unrecognized cause which killed off the worms is unknown, but they disappeared. The next year a few lice were found in one small cotton field but no where else, and on March 18, 1852, Davis happily recorded that "the lice have done much injury to the cotton around but have not hurt us."

shall Book: Household Hints," *The Alabama Historical Quarterly*, II (Fall Issue, 1940), 318-330.

Afterwards, very few lice or worms appeared in his cotton. He took pride in this outcome, and in 1858, when cotton worms were devastating cotton crops in the cane brake region of Alabama, expressed the belief that the ravage was caused by the failure of the cane brake planters to follow a rotation system of planting crops. Moreover, he remarked that they insisted on putting all of their land in cotton year after year, that they planted too closely, and that although their lands yielded much "vegetable matter" it brought very little "fruit," that is, cotton. His conclusion was that the cane brake planters and farmers should do as he had done in the meantime—turn at least partially to the production of corn and fodder rather than to continue to attempt to raise nothing but cotton.

Meantime, no sooner had Davis conquered the cotton worm and lice than he had to fight other pests which were destroying his crops. During his first years at Beaver Bend he was even bothered with the destruction of cotton by his hogs. On July 11, 1850, he made the following statement concerning this matter: "two pigs weighing 15 or 20 lbs. are Still in the lot & cotton field, Still in the Cotton & eating it. . . . These pigs have destroyed Cotton to the value of 20 or 30 dollars & might be Stopped out nearly as easy as calves. They Should be put into a clean pen & kept there *provided one can be made to hold them.* I cant understand the Economy of this. I want to raise hogs & cotton but they dont grow well together." On July 30, 1853 he found that weevils were eating his grain after it had been stored in bins and barns. His solution was to "Spread over & mix in the grain the leaves of the China, or Sassafras tree." While his wheat crop was in the field in 1852, it was partially destroyed by birds. On October 31, 1853, in order to prevent a recurrence of the loss, he prepared his wheat before sowing it by soaking "the Seed in Blue Vitriol, 1 hour, putting two tea Spoons full to the bushel—dried off with lime." Then, in 1854 and in 1855, before planting his corn it was rubbed with tar and ashes to keep off birds and worms. In the latter year he was bothered with grasshoppers, but did nothing to kill them off. Ashes were placed on watermelon hills to stop the ravages of bugs and, in 1857, in desperation, corn was planted early in order to prevent damage by cut worms. But Davis stated that even this was a vain hope. His last reference in his farm book to the subject of parasites was made on June 19, 1860, when he remarked that "The Beaver, Coon & Squirrels are playing havoc with the corn. . . ." As far as is known, this age-old problem of the farmer was always with Davis and although numerous efforts were made to solve it he never quite succeeded.

Another aspect of his management of Beaver Bend was his efforts to protect his crops from frosts. Again he employed some of the practices usually tried by his contemporaries and some which are followed by people living today in his region. In April, 1853, after a heavy frost had come to Beaver Bend, he covered his Irish potatoes with dirt to protect them. During April of the next year, when one of the heaviest frosts of the ante-bellum period threatened to destroy his entire corn crop, he covered some of his plants with dirt and when this seemed to show little prospects of success he spread all of his surplus cotton seed over his corn lands. The frost was so severe that he also decided to take precautions to save his cotton crop. On April 17, about forty acres of cotton land were covered with dirt and in addition he set fire to stumps and trees in the river bottom, "with the view of preventing frost from killing his cotton." As he stated, it was necessary to follow this unusual method because he had spread all of his unused cotton seed over his corn in order to protect the latter crop. He thought, too, that it was essential to do something to protect his cotton already planted. If it were killed by the frost he would be compelled to purchase cotton seed for re-planting purposes. Two days later he pessimistically recorded that his cotton had been "very badly plowed up in the effort to cover—this and the . . . frost and the mules feet have left the Chances for a Stand depending on the Seed yet to come up— The Corn where Covered Seems to have Suffered much less." As it happens, his pessimism was as usual unwarranted because his crops of 1854 were quite good. In 1855, he began to use leaves to protect Irish and sweet potatoes. Both were covered with cotton seed in 1857, but in 1858 leaves were employed once more. By 1860 he was utilizing pine straw, corn stalks and dirt as safeguards against frost.

Of all his quasi- and scientific experiments, Davis' most interesting were his tests of numerous varieties of seeds of plants in order to determine which were the most useful. He consistently sought the variety of each plant which would best suit his purposes, both from the standpoint of productiveness and profit. In one year, for example, he planted four kinds of watermelons, designated by him as Ice, Rattlesnake, Mountain Sprout, and Sugar Melon. At another time, seven varieties of corn were planted in the same year. They were Mississippi, Yellow, Wyandotte, Canada Prolific, Sugar, Rare Ripe, and Common Corn. Numerous kinds of fruit trees were set out, and at an early date he began grafting trees of different types to each other. On November 27, 1851, there were "Set out . . . 32 Cherry grafts in Plumb stocks, Just above the root & covered graft one inch below ground— 3 . . . were set in roots." Fruit trees were often transplanted, this being particularly the case with fig and peach trees. Several varieties of apple and peach trees were cultivated. In one year three kinds of peach trees were set out, namely: Early White Nutmeg, Oconee Green, and Raiger June. At the same time Carters, Nickijack and Shockley varieties of apple trees were planted. As might be expected, however, Davis was mostly interested in cotton and his most extensive experiments were connected with it. In this connection, too, it might be stated that he not only experimented with various types of cotton until he found what he wanted, but he also constructed and operated his own gin, he soon learned that cotton grew best on sandy soils, and early in his career began rotating his cotton and corn. On March 4, 1852, for example, he "Commenced planting Corn in the Pond field & Gin field which was last year in Cotton." He was still rotating the two crops in 1861.

No definite information is available on the types of cotton planted by Davis during his first two years at Beaver Bend, his first reference to the matter being made in 1850. In that year he indicated that 172 acres had been put in cotton and that the acreage of his several varieties was as follows: seventy acres in Prout or Royal Cluster; thirty-seven in Tarver or old Sugar Loaf; fifty in old Petit Gulf; ten in new Sugar Loaf; and five acres, in new ground, in a mixture of old Petit Gulf and Prout. Since old seed was used it is probable that it had been saved from the cotton crop of 1849, and if this was the case it may be assumed that among the varieties planted in 1849 were Sugar Loaf and Petit Gulf. After the 1850 cotton was planted a careful check was kept on the growth of the several varieties, and on July 11, Davis entered in his farm book, "The Cotton is very fine in appearance. The prout cotton exhibits a great many Suckers or extra limbs. It looks well, but I fear it is too leafy—look to this & consider the result. The Tarver & the new Sugar loaf present a clean limb & Strait Stocks. I have a fine opportunity to test these varieties & ascertain the better kind." Later a drought occurred in Perry County and in reporting on the effects of the dry weather on his cotton Davis made the observation on August 19, that "The Petit Gulf cotton has Stood the dry weather much better than the Prout or Sugar Loaf. This is plain: it is Still growing & fruiting, is much taller & promises to exceed either in production. This change has been rapid & unexpected, as at one time it was far behind the other varieties. Let the result be tested by the balances." On October 1, while testing the speed of his gin, still more was learned about the relative value of the varieties of cotton: "This day tested the Speed of my gin—She ginned 100 lbs. in 9 minutes ordinary pace of mules—This will give about 6,666 lbs per day of 10 hours; Also tested the percent of nett cotton, by weighing the Seed. Result 73 lbs. Seed from 100 lbs. gross—Tarver Cotton." Next day all three varieties were tested. Davis' description was, "This day Experimented with the varieties of Cotton. Result Prout 31¼ [from 100 lbs. gross]. Petit Gulf 30¼. Tarver 28¾. Subject to ¾ pound each for moats."

It was thus learned that the Tarver, or Sugar Loaf, seed produced less lint cotton than any of the three planted in 1850. But for some reason it was planted, along with the others, until 1854. Perhaps Davis was not fully satisfied with his tests. In 1851, he planted 173 acres of cotton, one acre less than in 1850. The fields, varieties of cotton, and acreage of each variety are indicated by the following table:

Field	Acres	Variety
Pond	40	Prout
Gin	52	Petit Gulf
Negro patches	9	Petit Gulf
Mulberry	30	Tarver
River Cut	10	Prout
Bayou Cut	20	Sugar Loaf
Reed Brake Cut	12	Sugar Loaf

In 1852, Petit Gulf was planted in several fields; Tarver was put in some newly cleared land; a new variety known as Pomegrante was tried out in two new fields; and a mixture of Tarver and Prout was planted in one small field. The next year Petit Gulf was planted in the largest fields, while Tarver was tried for the last time in one very small field. A new variety, Golden Chaff, was planted in three large fields; and another new kind, Willow, was put in a corner of a small field. In 1854, Davis turned away from all of the varieties he had tried out before 1853, except Petit Gulf; and the Golden Chaff had proved so productive in 1853 that it now became the standby. As recorded on April 5, 1854, "We planted the Golden Ch. in all the fresh land Except the B[each] Hammock [field] which is in the Willow Seed—The Mulberry field is in Petit Gulf except the half next the Corn—where the Golden Chaff is." As far as is known, these three varieties, especially Golden Chaff and Petit Gulf, were planted at Beaver Bend from 1854 until Davis' death in 1862. A variety of cotton known as Dean was planted in Davis' neighborhood as early as 1855, but, in 1856, after examining one of his friends' Dean cotton he concluded that it was not as good as Golden Chaff. In the matter of a summary, it may be pointed out that Prout, Tarver and Petit Gulf seed were planted exclusively at Beaver Bend in 1850 and 1851; Pomegrante was added in 1852; Prout and Pomegrante were eliminated and Golden Chaff and Willow were added in 1853; Tarver was eliminated in 1854; and after 1854, Golden Chaff, Petit Gulf and Willow, in the order of their importance, were cultivated.

_____ 3

PLANTATION MANAGEMENT: THE OVERSEER

O NE OF THE CHIEF PRACTICES of Southern planters in the period
before the Civil War was the delegation of partial supervision
of their agricultural enterprises into the hands of agents designated as overseers. Since Alabama became the leading cotton growing
state of the Old South for several years and because of the extensive
use there of the overseer system of cotton production on the large
plantations, the overseer may correctly be considered as one of the most
important figures in the ante-bellum agricultural history of the state.[1]
The fact that overseers helped in the management of Southern plantations does not mean, however, that the planters themselves took no
active part in directing the work on their places. Planters were usually
active in the conduct of their plantation affairs, whether they owned
large or small numbers of acres, or held limited or extensive numbers
of slaves. Most of them lived on or near their plantations and were
usually engaged, in cooperation with an overseer, if their places were
large enough to warrant such an agent, in operating their establishments. Only in scattered cases did the large planter-owner act as the
sole director of the affairs of his plantation.

The usual arrangement was one of joint directorship by the owner

[1]Davis, *The Cotton Kingdom in Alabama*, pp. 46-55, contains a discussion of the
general features of the plantation overseer system in Alabama in the ante-bellum period.

and his overseer. Ordinarily the owner lived on his place or in a nearby town, hired an overseer, instructed and supervised that person's activities, and held him responsible for all his actions, however important or seemingly trivial. If the owner happened to operate several plantations, or lived in a region some distance from his plantation, it was then necessary to delegate rather extensive powers to the overseers, but even then they were responsible to the absentee owner for all work carried on at the places over which they had control. In Alabama, as elsewhere in the South, the important function of the plantation overseer was to serve as director of the slaves and of the general activities on the place owned by his planter-boss. It was expected also that some profits should result for the owner from the overseer's work during each year. Because of the great authority with which the owner sometimes intrusted his overseer, the success or failure of the particular plantation under the overseer's direction often depended almost entirely upon the latter's own judgment and experience and upon the attention and care which he gave to the work being done by himself and by the slaves. These matters and the general historical and economic importance of the Southern ante-bellum overseer have been admirably presented elsewhere.[2] The purpose here is to mention briefly his general importance and the work done by him in Alabama and then to discuss in some detail some of the features of the activities of the overseers who worked for Hugh Davis at Beaver Bend.

It is generally recognized that Southern overseers in the years before 1861 were employed especially because the southern land-owning planters wished to be partially relieved from the tedious, daily task of supervising the work of their slaves. It was particularly for this job of directing the Negroes in their daily activities that overseers were hired. But only in very exceptional cases did a planter turn over complete supervision of a plantation to an overseer. Rarely did an overseer even have the privilege of purchasing plantation supplies and then only when directed by the planter to do so on a particular occasion. It was also indeed rare for an overseer to purchase a slave for his planter-employer. His important function, it should be reiterated, was to supervise everyday plantation work and to control the slaves in the name of the owner. From this standpoint, as in others, Beaver Bend was typical of the places operated in the Alabama blackbelt before 1861. In fact, on

[2]Ulrich B. Phillips, *Life and Labor in the Old South* (Boston, 1929).

June 17, 1854, after five and a half years at Beaver Bend, Davis informed the man who was then working as overseer that "An overseer is only wanted, because the negroes can't be trusted." This statement as much as any found concerning the overseers who worked for him demonstrates Davis' attitude toward his agents, and it may be taken as representative of the feelings of the planters of the Alabama black-belt and vicinity.

Of particular interest also is the question of the social position which the overseer held in southern ante-bellum society. Offhand, it may be stated if he were a professional overseer, that is, one who followed overseeing as an occupation, his position was not at all an enviable one. On the plantation where he worked he found himself placed socially somewhere between the Negro slaves and the owner and the members of the latter's family. He could associate intimately with neither group. In southern society generally he occupied a position between that of a free Negro and the large class of rural white non-slave-owners. Perhaps he should be placed in the latter group, although it should be added that many of the group would not have recognized him as their equal. Because of the rather strict caste system which existed, he had few intimate friends. He was certainly above the "poor-white" class, so-called, although they would not grant it, but was not as high in the social and economic scale as the group of white non-slaveholders who held land.

This latter group, by the way, seems to have made up the greatest portion of the southern white population by the late ante-bellum period. This class of society has lately attracted much attention among students of Southern history, and one of the South's leading historians has selected Perry County, Davis' home, as a typical Alabama blackbelt county. In 1850, eighty-four per cent of the farm population in the county owned land, and in 1860, land was owned by seventy-nine per cent of the group.[3] One could not belong to this stable class as long as he was a non-landowning overseer. The overseer being a white could not have too many contacts, except on business, with the Negroes in his charge. At the same time he was not accepted as a social equal by the other whites on the plantation where he happened to be working.

[3]Frank L. and Harriet C. Owsley, "The Economic Basis of Society in the late Ante-Bellum South," *Journal of Southern History*, VI (February, 1940), 32. This article contains a discussion of a new interpretation of the question of social classes in the South. Unpublished census reports of the Federal Government furnish most of the material used in the study by the authors.

If he were a bachelor he could at least, in some cases, eat some of his meals at the table of the planter, but even so he could not expect too many amenities while in the presence of the members of the planter's family. An illustration of this condition is shown by the following entry which an overseer made in a Davis farm book, late in the ante-bellum period, on January 31, 1858: "Mr. Jones & family, Miss Marshall, & Mr. Woodward dined with Mr. Davis. Miss Marshall is a nice young lady. Was at the table with her today twice & in the Parlor tonight & received no introduction to her." Such an incident is good evidence of one of the heaviest prices a man had to pay when he be-came an overseer.

From the standpoint of the planter, probably the worst feature of the overseer system was the eternal shifting about from plantation to plan-tation by the men who followed the occupation. In many cases no sooner had a planter instructed and trained a man in certain desired methods of plantation management than the overseer quit his job, either to accept another one or to take a rest—or to see the other side of the hill. It often happened that after a man moved into a particular re-gion, perhaps a county, and proved himself to be an efficient overseer, his original employer had difficulty in keeping him because other planters in the neighborhood came forward with offers of a higher salary. It most cases of this sort the overseer eagerly accepted the newly offered position. This was especially true whenever the over-seer had no particular friendly attachments for his planter-employer; and for several reasons he failed in many instances to develop any great loyalty toward his employer. He had to execute the owner's every wish and desire, and had little opportunity for redress of real or supposed grievances because of his position as a quasi-menial. His main defense when he became dissatisfied with a job was to quit, but then he was faced with the problem of obtaining another job. His position usually afforded little security because he could be fired at any moment by his employer; thus he held merely the position of a hired man almost en-tirely at the mercy of the planter. His important problem as a pro-fessional overseer was to locate some planter who would respect him for his ability; and it is perhaps for this reason as much as any other, in addition to the desire to obtain some security, that the southern over-seer seems so often to have been on the move from one plantation to another. Sometimes the overseer found such a planter; then relations between the two men were almost those of equals, at least as far as the business operation of the plantation was concerned. On the other hand, it was quite unusual for an overseer to find a southern planter who considered him as a social equal, even if that planter himself had risen from the position of an overseer. All in all, the position of the southern overseer was desirable neither from a social nor an economic standpoint.

In his relations with the various Beaver Bend overseers, Hugh Davis followed the usual practices of the planters of his region and period. Because of his training as a lawyer he was careful to work out an elaborate collection of rules which he required his overseers to follow in their direction of activities at Beaver Bend. The rules were written in the various farm books which were kept throughout Davis' management of his place, and it was emphatically ordered that the overseers always conform to the rules. Davis always considered this conformity to his regulations as one of the most important duties of his overseers, and in this respect he was as strict as any planter in the region known to the present writer. As has been pointed out in a previous place, one of Davis' first acts in 1848 was to draw up what he called "GEN-ERAL RULES & DIRECTIONS EVERY YEAR" and "Special Rules to the Overseer." The "Special Rules" enumerated briefly the duties of the overseer, and are of special importance because it was under them, primarily, that Beaver Bend was operated by the overseers from January 1, 1848, until June, 1854. At the latter date a more elaborate group of rules was established.

As might be expected, most of the 1848 rules concerned the overseer's management of slaves on the plantation; and it is thought best to in-clude them in a later discussion of the position of Negroes at Beaver Bend. Consequently, only those rules which specifically concern the general duties of the overseer are mentioned here. He had to give particular attention to the care of stock; and when the slaves were feed-ing, currying, rubbing, or washing the teams, the work was supervised by him "unless a good Excuse exists." It was required, too, that the overseer make certain at all times that no food for animals was left in troughs or racks after feeding time, but "put away carefully for next time." He was to see that no fences were damaged, "nor any rails left lying down when accidently off." All gates were kept closed, and no stock of any kind were allowed to run in the feed lot or stables. All mending and repairing of plantation equipment was done at the earliest possible moment convenient after the damages were noticed, or called to the attention of the overseer. If a slave refused more than once to cooperate in observing these rules, he was to be "punished with Stripes" by the overseer. In concluding his special instructions Davis ruled that his agent should be dismissed for neglecting his duties. As Davis was still living in Marion at the time, he added, "When the employer has observed a violation of these rules at two successive weekly visits it is understood that . . . the overseer knows, or has observed, it & approves it, & is answerable for it."

Davis' next set of rules for his overseers is to be found in his farm book under the date of June 17, 1854, and this group is of special significance for several reasons. The new orders were established at a time just after great difficulties had been had with overseers; as a matter of fact, during the preceding six months three overseers had worked at Beaver Bend and none of them had been satisfactory. Thus the rules set up after the departure of the three men perhaps indicate the failings of those particular overseers and point out precisely the functions which they had been failing to perform properly. The rules demonstrate, moreover, that Davis had acquired a more detailed, intimate knowledge of the actual conduct of plantation management since he had moved to Beaver Bend in December, 1851. Furthermore, the regulations are pertinent particularly for the information they contain concerning a typical day's activities of a Beaver Bend overseer during the spring and summer months, the busiest seasons of the year on the plantation. Davis entered them in his farm book under the heading of "Rules & Directions to my overseer by which to give Satisfaction & earn Wages, daily." As in the case of most of the Beaver Bend rules and regulations and of the ordinary activities of other persons connected with the plantation, these show that the daily work of Davis' overseers was typical of others of the same occupation in and near the Alabama blackbelt.

The overseer's first duty of the day was to "Rise and blow his horn by daylight & not after." As soon as the Negroes were dressed and ready for work, he was to accompany either the hoe hands or the plow hands to their place of work, see that they began their task correctly, and "then take breakfast—either at the house or in the field as Suits his work best." After breakfast the overseer went to the place where the hoe hands were working, checked each row which had been cleaned of weeds and grass, and either himself or a slave under his direction pulled up any growths which the hoe hands might have neglected to destroy. If a row had been left "foul" by a Negro, that Negro had to answer for his negligence to the overseer. About eleven o'clock in the morning the overseer left the hoe hands and visited the plow hands in order to examine their work carefully. He made certain that the rows were being plowed as Davis had directed and that the furrows were "Straight & the land thoroughly plowed." He stayed with the plow hands until twelve o'clock noon. During the noon recess, he examined each mule, its gear, collars, and especially its shoulders in order to ascertain if the animal was in physical shape to work. If an animal had developed the colic it was given a mint tea until relief was obtained. At feeding time the overseer unlocked the crib, gave out the feed, relocked the crib doors, and went to the stables where he examined all troughs and stalls and made certain that they were clean before food was placed in them for the animals. The overseer ate his noon meal with the plow hands, and afterwards returned to the stables where he supervised other slaves while they were currying the mules and horses. Then, after directing the gearing and harnessing of the animals for the afternoon's work, he returned to the fields with the plow hands and started them off again. When this task was done he went once more to the hoe hands and remained with them until dark, except for one afternoon visit with the plow hands. This special attention accorded the hoes seems to show that Davis, similar to most planters in his region, considered hoe work as the most important in preparing a crop. If the mules needed any special attention during any part of the day, the overseer attended to them. At night he unlocked the crib, once more gave out food for the animals, saw them dressed off, locked the crib, took his own supper, and made entries of the day's work in the farm book. At nine o'clock he blew his horn, checked on the presence of the slaves, and immediately afterwards retired for the night.

In addition to the above list of regular, daily activities, the rules also included directions for the performance of several other duties required of the overseer. In no case was he to stop a Negro at a plow or hoe in order "to attend to Small extra jobs which he [the overseer] has Skill or Strength to do himself." He should never neglect his own work in order to talk to persons who happened to be passing along the road, nor "Set upon the fence whilst his hands are at work—nor get into the Shade of a tree to avoid the SunShine." It was added that "These practices are common enough with the younger portion of overseers, but are a disgrace to a business man." Every article belonging to the plantation was to be carefully preserved and as Davis put it, "The Owner may give, but the overseer must deny." It was also specified that only the overseer, never a Negro, should exercise control over the slaves. None of the authority given the overseer could be delegated by him to any Negro. In performing duties and in all actions on the plantation Davis advised his overseer to strive to hide his faults from the slaves, "but if not possible then never in any event whatever request or require the negroes to conceal his faults from the employer—In Such case the overseer is unmanned—better to retire at once from a place he can but disgrace, when afraid his hands may tell on him." For conscientious attention to duty the overseer was to be rewarded. For every theft of pigs, chickens, or other articles committed by a Negro which he discovered and reported he received a payment of fifty cents. Besides, if he continued to work on the plantation until the end of the year during which he started, he was paid fifty cents for each one hundred pounds of pork made "by his own attention & care." At no time, however, was a Beaver Bend overseer allowed to share in the cotton crop of the place, nor was he ever paid on the basis of cotton bales produced.

A habit acquired by Davis while he was practicing law comes in good stead in adding to the knowledge of the duties he required of his overseers. Being a lawyer he was accustomed to write out or to approve of written documents and contracts of his clients. When he became a planter he very naturally drew and signed contracts with his overseers. As early as October 14, 1851, he refers in his farm book to a written contract with an overseer named Mathew C. Wells. On August 7, 1852, Wells signed another contract which, by the way, provided for an increase in salary of fifty dollars. In 1853, another contract is mentioned. Davis' last contract with an overseer was signed in April, 1861. Thus, it may be assumed that some sort of written agreement was made every year. Possession of copies of these contracts of course adds more information about Davis' relations with his agents, as well as the requirements he established for their conduct of activities at Beaver Bend. In keeping with his legal background, too, he even made and retained several copies of each contract. A few copies of such agreements and one original have been located. The original one is quoted in its entirety here. It was signed in 1856, and may be accepted as an indication of the requirements established that year for the guidance of the overseer at the plantation. Of equal importance also is the reference to the agent's special privileges. The contract was as follows:

Articles of agreement made and entered into between Hugh Davis on the one part and Thomas J. Parnell both now in the County of Perry—Witness that Said Davis doth hereby agree to engage the services of said Parnell to oversee and manage his plantation, negroes & business of Planting on & near the Cahaba River, whereon Said Davis now resides under Such Rules & regulations as Said Davis may prescribe & direct from time to time, for and during the year A. D. 1857, unless this Contract is ended before the end of Said year according to a Stipulation to be inserted herein after—at & for the Sum of Three Hundred & fifty Dollars to be at the end of Said year in cash paid with also Three Hundred pounds of Pork-Meat for the use of Said Parnells family & so much meal as may be necessary & proper for Supplying Said Family with bread during the time he may be so employed as Such Overseer.

Article 2d. It is further contracted and agreed that the cooking for said Parnells family Shall & may be done by the Plantation Cook of Said Davis, but it is also agreed that after the cooking is done, the Said Parnell is to have the provisions carried to his table & his table Services done by Servants of his own providing—as also all the Services of his housekeeping.

Article 3. It is further agreed that the washing for Said Parnells family Shall be done by Said Plantation Cook, also the ironing—The washing and Ironing of plain Clothes is here meant & for fine Clothes the washing & Ironing is not provided to be done by Said Davis or Said Cook.

Article 4. Said Davis contracts for no regular kept horse for Said Parnell to ride, but agrees that for necessary riding about the plantation the Said Parnell may use a horse, Whenever not required to be in the plow, or other plantation work—and also may use Such horse in going to Church from time to time.

Article 5. Said Parnell engages to give his attention & Care faithfully to the duties of overseer on Said plantation—in caring for the Slaves—the Stock of all kinds—The utensils of the farm & the provisions to be used on the place—using his best Skill and endeavours to promote the interest & welfare of Said Davis whilst So engaged.

Article 6. And it is hereby Stipulated & agreed that either one of the Said parties hereto, may whenever he becomes dis[s]atisfied in his mind & that it is for his interest & advantage to put an end to this agreement the Same Shall be ended & closed upon one days notices given for that object & the Services on the one part & the wages on the other Shall no longer be required or exacted by either party of the other.

Article 7. It is further hereby promised and agreed by Said Davis that he will pay to Said Parnell for Said Services the Said Sum of Three Hundred & fifty Dollars in money payable the first day of Jany 1858. That he will provide Said Parnells family three hundred pounds of Pork—and Supply them with bread during the year 1857 if this Contract Continues in force during that time and a place to live in, being the House now on the place known as the overseers house.

Article 8. It is further agreed that this Contract Shall be Signed by the parties
hereto & then left with Mr. O. T. Jones, who will give copies to either party on request. Given under our hands & Seals this 20th day of Oct 1856.

HUGH DAVIS
THOMAS J. PARNELL

Teste

H. HOLMES

Although the form of this contract differs somewhat from the specific rules which had been established both in 1848 and in 1854, it does
demonstrate precisely the special privileges which Davis allowed his
overseer and it includes in a general way some of the duties expected of
him. It is quite obvious, too, that the overseer at this time was expected to follow both the rules of 1848 and 1854, as well as conform
to the above contract. The next set of rules was announced as January
3, 1861. At that time, however, the overseer was merely informed once
more that he was to rise and "blow a horn or ring a bell at day light for
all hands to rise and prepare for work as early as there is sufficient
light." It was also reiterated that he should start the Negroes off "for
a good days work; . . . [and inspect] all provision troughs & have them
kept well clean." Then after listing several regulations for the slaves,
which will be discussed at a latter point, Davis reminded his overseer
that he was to blow a horn also at nine o'clock in the evening, at which
time the slaves were to retire.

These were the last rules set down by Davis before the outbreak of
the Civil War, although on March 4, 1861, he did once more call an
overseer's attention to the rules which had earlier been drawn up for
his and his predecessors' observance. The overseer was instructed to
read every rule which had been established at Beaver Bend since 1848,
and this shows that Davis, as late as the month before the War began,
still believed that his original rules of 1848 were acceptable in the operation of his plantation. He thus evolved a system of operation throughout his entire career as owner of Beaver Bend. Successive rules did not
necessarily supercede previous ones, but were established mainly to em-
phasize in more minute detail certain aspects of plantation operation.
Davis naturally learned more of management the longer he operated
his place. Rules for his overseers and his whole system of farming
were of an accumulative nature. Finally, on June 1, 1862, less than a
week before his death, he wrote down his most elaborate set of rules.
They represent a cumulated knowledge gained from fourteen and a

half years experience as a planter and for that reason are of particular significance.

This last collection of rules not only included a list of the jobs to be performed by the overseer, but also referred to the functions of every person connected with the work at the plantation. As previously mentioned, it was designated by Davis as his "System of farming at Beaver Bend."[4] The most important task of the overseer, as pointed out by Davis, "was to keep all the rules and enforce them on the place and see that the regulations [concerning the slaves] are carried out." The overseer was expected "to use his best skill and ability to accomplish the purposes of the employer," and in fulfilling this requirement was particularly required to learn all the rules and regulations, "so as to understand and believe in them to which end they are recorded in the farm books." He was instructed to lock all houses in which stock, provisions and tools were kept, and no Negro was to be allowed access to any keys of the plantation outhouses or buildings. Another duty was "to see that all things of value to the master shall be preserved scrupulously." Among the articles specifically listed under this heading were: mealbags, spinning cotton, extra tools not in use, iron, coal, peas, rice, broom corn, wagon gear, and cotton sacks. In this connection, Davis also restated an earlier maxim that "an agent may give liberally of his, but should be stingy with what belongs to his employers." He repeated too, that any time after the overseer began working at the plantation, either he or his employer could dissolve the contract which had been signed. But it was added that the wages to be paid the overseer were not due, under any circumstances, until January 1, following the year for which the contract had been signed. He was encouraged to ask questions freely at all times of the owner in regard to the methods of farming being practiced at Beaver Bend. He had to learn all of the rules in force and agree to observe them faithfully. He should resign his job immediately if he could not follow the rules. If he lost any time from his work either because of sickness or other cause, thus forcing the owner to hire a substitute, his salary was to be docked for each day he was unable to superintend the affairs of the plantation.

Continuing with his rules, Davis intrusted the overseer with a number of general duties. Of special importance was the power of enforcing

[4]See Weymouth T. Jordan, " 'System of Farming at Beaver Bend,' Alabama, 1862," *Journal of Southern History,* VII (February, 1941), 76-84.

all discipline and punishment of the Negroes at Beaver Bend. It was stated once more, too, that no slave should have any privileges or authority over another one. The overseer was cautioned that "all punishment should be administered for the purpose of humane discipline and free from passion." Whenever a slave became ill, his case was to be reported to the owner, but the overseer was to attend the Negro during his illness. It was expected that the overseer be familiar with the various common ailments most often prevalent among Negro slaves and know methods of treating them. To reduce the hazard of fire, only the owner and the overseer were allowed to carry a lantern or torch into the gin-house or other buildings which were liable to take fire easily. The overseer repaired all breakage of tools and equipment on the day during which the damage occurred, in order that the implements might be used the next day. Every valuable tool had its proper place of storage and was kept there under his direction. After each year's crops had been laid by for the season, he supervised the Negroes in their destruction of pests and growths which were harmful, especially such "troublesome growths as come up and mature before frost, such as chicken corn, sheep burrs, morning glories and such like." A most important job was attending to feeding the stock and examining carefully every day its condition, the examination taking place during the hour immediately after breakfast. Throughout the year he divided the Negroes into as many squads as there were daily divisions of work and appointed a leader of each squad. Each leader was held responsible for his squad's work and made nightly reports to the overseer. A final function of the overseer was the general supervision of the work of the plantation cook, who usually prepared the food for everyone at Beaver Bend except for the owner's family.

Of these rules Davis was most insistent, as always, that his overseers learn the general requirements established for the operation of the plantation and that the rules be learned or memorized and adhered to consistently. Davis had always expected his agents to follow his rules and whenever it seemed to him that they were neglecting their duties they were immediately referred to the rules. He was especially demanding in this respect after he became paralyzed in June, 1859, because afterwards he was usually indoors and his only reliable method of checking on the work being done at the plantation was to read over the entries which his overseer was making in his farm books. One important rule was to the effect that complete records should be kept. On one occasion in particular, in 1861, he became exceedingly irked when he noticed that his overseer was not conforming to this rule. The overseer, named A. P. Green, had recorded, on February 9, that he had "cleaned out part of the Ditches." Davis wrote the word "what" beside the entry. Green had written that he had "Repaired Sum fence." Davis inquired "where." "Sum manure" had been hauled. Davis asked "how much." His dissatisfaction was expressed again on March 4. On this date Green entered in the farm book that several Negroes "went over about two acres [of corn] which we had planted a week ago and covered the cotton Seed." Davis had earlier instructed that the seed be placed around the corn hills as fertilizer and that it be allowed to remain there above the ground. He was infuriated at Green's action and informed him sarcastically that it was "not authorized," and instructed him to read carefully all of the rules which had been established since 1848, referring him to the specific pages of the farm books where each set of rules could be found.

Now that reference has been made to all of the rules worked out at Beaver Bend for the guidance of the overseers, a discussion of the various overseers and of Davis' relations with them and their observance of the rules, as well as something of the work which they accomplished, seems to be in order. The first overseer, starting in January, 1848, was a man named Joseph Pitts. As it happens, however, the only definite information which has been located concerning Pitts is that he was paid a salary of three hundred dollars for the year and that he was dismissed in December, 1848, because he did not suit Davis. On September 22, Davis had received the following letter from an applicant for Pitt's job: "I understand that you wish to employ me to Oversee for you for the ensuing year—If you do want me as such you can get me by paying me $200.00. Please write me by mondays mail. I am anxious to hear from you, as I expect Some other offers." The letter was signed by a man by the name of Daniel M. Day. This solicitous applicant was not hired, however, and the position was filled at the beginning of 1849 by an overseer, John R. Wright, who went to Beaver Bend and remained there for two entire years. For a year and a half Wright performed his work in a most acceptable manner, but by the summer of 1850 it became evident that he was neglecting his duties. On June 22, 1850, Davis noticed that "There is Some grass in the bottom &

portions of the new ground suffering for plowing & hoeing very much. Horses and mules exhibit great want of food, water and attention. I have Seldom any where Seen a team in so unsightly a fix." Four days later he complained of "Mules in oat Field—This is doing harm to my hogs. My hogs in the Stable & feed lots. This is improper." On June 28, he again fumed, "Came down—Mr. Wright absent—fishing— wrote him a letter complaining of his absence & management on several particulars." With so many faults it is surprising that Wright was not fired outright, but for some reason he was allowed to finish out the year. The farm book, December 30, states that Davis "Came down & put hands under new overseer."

Beginning with the year 1851, Davis made more frequent visits to Beaver Bend and under his more personal direction the plantation was operated during 1851-1853 by two men, Pleasant C. Harris and Mathew C. Wells. Harris worked from January 1 to October 13, 1851, and was paid on the basis of $225 a year. That he was dismissed in October, at the time when cotton was being picked, indicates that he, too, had become entirely unsatisfactory. Davis supplies no information why he let Harris go, however. Mathew C. Wells, Harris' successor, began work the day the latter was released and continued with Davis until the end of 1853. Wells turned out to be one of the best overseers at Beaver Bend in the years before the outbreak of the War. His salary for 1852 was three hundred dollars, and on August 7, 1852, he was rehired, with an increase in salary of fifty dollars, for the year 1853. He was not paid until December 31, 1853, however, on which date Davis wrote in his farm book, "I gave him my note for 652-Dollars for 2 Yrs overseeing payable 1 Jany 1855." Wells of course did not wait until 1855 to get his money, for he borrowed immediately on the note. His willingness to work for two years without pay and then to accept such a note shows that he and Davis were on splendid terms. He left Davis to go into business for himself. That he was satisfactory is shown also by the fact that he worked longer at the plantation than any other overseer during the entire period Davis operated it. Moreover, in the year following his departure, Davis had more difficulties with overseers than in any year between 1848 and 1862. Perhaps one reason for the difficulties was the failure to locate anyone who could compare favorably with Wells in ability.

During 1854, four men worked for Davis, three of them in the first half of the year, and even the last man hired was dismissed after working for a little more than seven months. James M. Gilbert started the year, but on January 16, Davis reported, "This morning Closed & turned off Mr. Gilbert, paid him 8.00 for 2 weeks." For a week Davis attended to affairs, but then complained, "I am outdone and want help." On January 24 a man named James M. Taylor was hired at $225 a year. Taylor began work immediately, but he soon proved so slow in performing as well as learning his duties that Davis tired of him also. He was replaced, on May 5, by a new man, Henry Kennedy. As Davis put it, Kennedy was paid the same as Taylor, "at 225$ a year—or 18.75 per month or 62 cts. a day—or 5 cents an hour." On this basis the overseer was thus expected to work twelve hours a day. It seemed that at last a man had been found who could perform his work in a satisfactory manner, and on May 15 it was recorded "This is the best days work in 3 years." A week later Davis rejoiced in the excellence of his new overseer with "Hurra for Taylor." Here he was either expressing happiness because Taylor was no longer with him, or had had so many overseers during the year that he had forgotten that Kennedy had replaced Taylor. But once more difficulties arose. On June 4, Kennedy asked for leave of absence to go home and help with the cotton crop on his father's farm nearby. The request was granted, but the next day Kennedy was paid off and fired for having left his job.

Again Davis looked after his business for a short period. Because of the numerous changes in overseers, however, work was lagging at the plantation. To rectify this, Davis determined, on June 6, "If the weather is good I have determined to get my Cotton to a Stand & my Corn laid bye if we have to work till 10 O'ck at night." Under this rule during the next week he finished more work than had been accomplished in one week "for years." On June 17, he once more found a man, J. A. Barnett, who seemed satisfactory as overseer. But Barnett stayed at Beaver Bend only until February 10, 1855. He was paid $225 a year, that is, at that rate. When he left he also received extra pay for having given special attention to the plantation hogs during his tenure. The settlement made at his departure seems to be worthy of special note. For services of six months and ten days Davis owed Barnett the sum of $119.90. For extra attention to hogs the overseer was due $12.50. For the one month and ten days work in

1855, $27.77 was owed but not due until January 1, 1856. When Barnett left he was paid $100 in cash, given a note of $32.40 payable on demand, and the promise of payment of the $27.77 on January 1, 1856. This arrangement is typical of hundreds made by Davis in the settlement of his plantation accounts.

Barnett was not dismissed as overseer because he had failed to perform his duties satisfactorily, but because Davis had decided to operate Beaver Bend without the aid of a white overseer. The arrangement he had hit upon was for himself to act as general director of activities and to appoint two of his most efficient Negroes as leaders possessing special powers. The two slaves selected as leaders were Wash and Young Sol, and Davis was willing to make the experiment of operating his place with these Negroes as assistants because they had earlier shown themselves to possess outstanding qualities. Both had lived and worked at Beaver Bend from 1848, and had shown themselves to be faithful in almost every respect. Wash had been acting as leader of the plow hands and had always conducted himself in a most acceptable manner. He was also an excellent carpenter. Young Sol was expert in numerous jobs and had the distinction of being able to perform more skilled jobs than any slave on the plantation. At different times between 1848 and 1861 he was a carriage driver, orchardist, blacksmith, and currier.

In the first week of February, 1855, when the decision was made of running his place with the assistance of the two Negroes, Davis worked out some special rules for their guidance: "I propose to make the crop of 1855 without an overseer and try my men Wash & Sol as leaders & reporters of Conduct & I intend to reward or punish them for good or evil behaviour differently from the other hands. . . ." Wash was appointed leader of the slaves when all of them worked together. When they were divided into gangs he acted as leader of the hoes, while Young Sol directed the work of the plow hands. During the time of the experiment they received all orders from their master and merely executed orders, although they were allowed to use their discretion when not ordered specifically to perform a particular job. Wash kept the hoes in place and the hoe hands working and Young Sol maintained orderly conduct and work among the plow hands. Sol was charged with keeping the plows in repair and attending to the currying of the mules. Wash maintained the stables and stalls in good order. Together they attended to the corn stored in plantation cribs. Each had authority to prevent other slaves from leaving the place unless their master had given special permission to go.

Under this system of management, Beaver Bend had two of its most successful years. But for Davis it had its drawback, for he had to remain almost always at or near the plantation. The successes of 1855 and 1856 may have been due for the most part to his presence, but some credit should go to his Negro leaders, too. A week after the new order was established Davis reported "Have overseed one week. . . . Stayed with plows most of the time & gone around to the others once a day." As a further check on Wash and Young Sol he determined also to "keep a list of the good & bad conduct of my leaders — & Shall reward the one with the first & highest reward who oftenest is found obeying my orders—I Shall also note down Each ones Short Comings in regard to things not ordered particularly." That the two Negroes were acceptable at their jobs is borne out by the fact that only three marks were placed beside their names during the next two years. Young Sol received only one black mark, for watering several of the plantation mules with bad water until it was harmful to their condition. Wash received two marks, one for having stayed in the woods one night, the other for being "caught asleep at the crib door." But at the same time both were rewarded for their good work, Sol being paid twenty-five dollars, while Wash got fifteen dollars. Part of Sol's reward came, however, for extra work done in the blacksmith shop.

Davis' immediate reaction to his new method of operation is best shown by his own description of work accomplished during the second month after the system was inaugurated. On March 31, 1855, he wrote in his farm book: "For work few March months ever equalled this. . . . I find that I plowed 25 days this month—and have prepared about 70 acres for corn and about 90 for cotton. . . . I confess that I am 1 week behind good farming in my plowing, yet I feel sure that my plantation was never in so good plight any year before—having regard to fences, ditches, ponds, Sloughs & gates — My Stock are in good order— . . . & but for cold weather, & its effects the planter would feel hopeful & glad." During December, 1855, Davis went on a trip to Mississippi to visit his parents, and while away the work of the plantation was continued under the direction of his Negro leaders.

Work went on as usual; the gin was operated, cotton picked, job work done in the blacksmith shop, spinning done by the slave women, and the slaves in general were kept busy with the many odd jobs always performed during the winter months. The only unusual feature of affairs at the plantation during the master's absence was the amount of illness among the Negroes. This of course may have been from natural causes, although it is more likely that the slaves were merely taking a rest from work while they had the opportunity. Even so, when Davis returned home on December 30, he found everyone in good health and of more importance stated that everything had apparently been well taken care of.

During 1856, he continued as his own overseer and retained his two Negroes in their positions as leaders. This in itself shows that he was satisfied with the set-up as it had been established in 1855. In April, 1856, he again went on a trip, leaving Beaver Bend in charge of Wash and Young Sol. This time he went on a short business trip to Mobile. On April 26, after his return he expressed his satisfaction with his Negro leaders' conduct of affairs while he had been away: "The hoes Spread the manure & kept up with the plows—I found the management in my absence good So far as I could look into it— There was no outbreaking conduct calling for punishment or even reproach." Next day after a more thorough examination he found everything "well," and on the following Saturday gave the Negroes a half holiday in appreciation and as a reward for their good work during his absence. The whole year 1856 went by satisfactorily as far as direction of work at Beaver Bend was concerned and on December 31, Davis rejoiced that his corn was plentiful and his meat "nearly so." His cotton was selling at a good price and his stock was in good order. Moreover, the size of the cotton crops in 1855 and 1856 shows that his place was managed quite successfully during the two years he dispensed with a hired overseer. In 1855, he made 135,659 pounds of seed cotton, or seventy-seven bales; and in 1856, seventy-six bales from 134,878 pounds. These two crops compared very favorably with those made in 1854 and 1857, the years before and after Davis and his Negroes directed affairs at the plantation. The entire amounts of land under cultivation in 1855 and 1856 are also pertinent, there being a steady increase over 1854. All this means that the experiment of operating without a hired white overseer was quite successful. Davis' part in these successes should not be minimized, however. In addition, he had saved the amount of money which ordinarily would have been paid out to an overseer. It may be concluded that he did not turn back to the usual method of operation in 1857 for a monetary reason. His main reason must have been a desire for more leisure time for himself. That he had indeed been satisfied with his Negro leaders in 1855 and 1856 is borne out also by the fact that during part of the year 1860 he again turned to the same two Negroes, and another one, for the direction of his plantation. This seems to be especially significant because at the latter date he was literally flat on his back because of paralysis, and had to depend more completely on his Negroes then than had been necessary in 1855 and 1856.

Davis' first choice of an overseer for 1857 was Thomas J. Parnell, whose contract has been quoted in full at an earlier point in this chapter. Parnell broke his contract, however, by not showing up for work, and Davis turned to a young man named Jesse Wells. It is believed that the new overseer was a relative of the Mathew C. Wells who had been overseer from October, 1851 through December, 1853. On January 5, 1857, Davis describes his arrangements with Jesse Wells. "Mr. Jesse Wells began to oversee for me this year on terms to be set forth in written agreement—in substance 175$ & if he continues till the end of the year, I gratuitously promise to allow him 50 cents on the hundred lbs. of meat." This salary represents a reduction of fifty dollars from the amount last paid an overseer, back in 1854, and a reduction of two hundred dollars from the offer made to Parnell. Wells got such a small salary because he was not required to perform all of the usual duties formerly expected of overseers. He at no time during his sojourn at Beaver Bend made an entry in the farm book, Davis reserving that function for himself. The only stock on the place with which he was concerned was the hogs. Wash and Young Sol continued to look after the other stock. Accordingly, Wells' important job was to direct the field work of the Negroes.

Under such conditions there is small wonder that Davis soon became somewhat dissatisfied with his new overseer, especially after the young man was allowed to take on a few extra jobs. On January 16, it was complained that Wells was cutting rails from the wrong stand of timber on the plantation, Davis remarking that "This comes from my being absent." Following numerous incidents of a similar nature Wells was finally dismissed on June 20, 1857, because, as Davis put it, the young man was not qualified "to manage for me." He did add, however, "Still I may go further & fare worse, but I really wish to be at liberty once and awhile & not be a perpetual Slave to my Slaves which I must ever be when my overseer has no experience."

Davis was here expressing the chief reason a planter of the ante-bellum South wanted a dependable overseer. But what else could he have expected when he hired an untried man in order to cut expenses? Certainly he could have found a more experienced person if he had looked hard enough. Now he had either to do his own work or find someone who was both competent and experienced and pay that person a fair wage. After three weeks he located and hired a man named R. H. Roark. Not much is known about the new overseer, except that during the short time he worked for Davis he was most efficient and directed the Negroes and the work on the plantation in a manner which was considered most gratifying. In order to obtain his services Davis had to pay $350 a year, which was the amount originally offered to Parnell. The salary paid was the highest yet given an overseer at Beaver Bend. Roark did not start to work until September 23, and then remained only until December 14, when he left "to Engage in business in Dallas [County]." This man was exceptional in numerous ways. He was one of the best overseers to work for Davis, and the only one who ever expressed a definite personal liking for his employer. Two days before leaving Beaver Bend, he wrote in the farm book: "The time is fast approximating when I must leave Mr. Davis for whom I have formed very great attachments."

After Roark's departure Davis was still determined to get a man who could run the plantation in such a way that the owner might have some freedom from petty details of management. At the beginning of the next year he hired an overseer who had formerly been employed by a neighboring planter. The man came with high recommendations, and was paid a salary of $350 a year. The new agent, John T. Tinsley, took over on January 3, 1858, and remained with Davis until October 24. From the beginning, however, the two men could not get along well together and it is really surprising that the overseer was retained for ten months. Davis' first displeasure was expressed on March 15, after a business trip to Memphis, Tennessee. He stated that in his absence "the work has gone on well—That is

much has been done," but added "its Style is no ways Superior— . . .
mules are not in as good order as I expected. . . ." Later, during one
of Davis' short absences Tinsley was partially responsible for the destruction of a large part of the plantation's fodder crop. The mishap
occurred on July 30, 1858, while the overseer was directing some of
the Negroes in the important job of pulling and stacking fodder.
While at their job the Negroes were forced to stop by a sudden downpour of rain. Some of the stacks of fodder were down, others were
scattered on the ground preparatory to stacking, and some had not
yet been gathered. The rain ruined a large part of the fodder. On
his return next day Davis attempted desperately to save part of his
soaked crop by "spreading, sunning, turning, hand stacking & stacking" it. He wrote scathingly in his farm book of the overseer's negligence:

This day Spent in the field examining my fodder & endeavouring to save it from
destruction—On Friday [July 30] we had a heavy rain & nearly all my new ground
fodder was caught & got very wet—3 Stacks wholly exposed—4 or 5 about halfway up—
one large Stack merely piled up. . . . This was a bad State of things & my best Skill
will be requisite to Save it in half Condition—I am utterly unable to account for
Such a Condition of things, & reproach myself for not having given more attention to
So important a Job. My plans were not duly impressed on Mr. Tinsley & his experience was too limited to enable him to accomplish the work—So much for my neglect
& absence from home—My fodder Saving is a failure—& my utmost endeavors will
Scarcely enable me to get through next Season—I must have 15,000 lbs. now in great
danger—It is burnt badly—pulled badly—tied badly—toted badly—Shocked Shockingly
—& Stacked far worse than any Similar work I ever Saw—It looked as if pulled before
day, tied up with the left hand—toted through the corn in a run & Stacked in the
darkness of midnight—It has been wet twice & Stands a fair chance either to rot down-
right or to be too full of Sand for the mules teeth so I conclude to write the word
Failur[e] against my fodder crop. . . .

This biting criticism of Tinsley's work was continued two days later,
when Davis wrote further about the matter in his farm book, a place
where the overseer could not help but see it, "Examined the fodder
Stacked up Saturday [July 31]—decided to let it Stand for the
present—made air vents on each Side to let heat escape. . . . The result of today Shows how important it is to keep from dropping a
Stitch in one's operations. . . . Catch me asleep again if possible."
He did indeed keep a close eye on affairs during the rest of Tinsley's
tenure as overseer. This is evidenced by a remark made on August 28,
while he was supervising the construction of a stable, to the effect that
his "presence was needed every moment," for whenever he was absent

his "work went wrong." But this attention did not save his fodder crop, and for once his pessimism was justified. His total fodder from 150 acres of corn amounted to only twenty-six loads or stacks. As a result he was compelled to use peanut and pea vines as fodder to a greater extent than usual in feeding his stock during the fall and winter of 1858.

Davis had still another complaint to make concerning Tinsley's management. It seems that during his stay at Beaver Bend the overseer neglected to attend to the task of filling places on the plantation which had been washed by rain. At a later time Davis in derision dubbed the eroded places as "Tinsley gullies" in dubious honor of the overseer. As might be expected, in view of the unpleasant incidents which occurred while Tinsley was with Davis, their association terminated in a most unusual manner. On October 24, 1858, Tinsley wrote Davis a letter of resignation. The letter is self-explanatory:

> Mr. Davis Esq. Respect Sir. I have after three months deliberate consideration determined to withdraw from your employment. I have a number of good reasons for so doing, Two of which I will give. 1st your great unnecessity for an overseer, so long as you have Wash, Solomon, George, Johnson & Poldo—Again, your great Tendency to become excited & absence of mind while excited. I shall go up next Wednesday for a settlement very Respect. J. T. TINSLEY

The letter was handed to Davis on the day it was written. The "three months deliberate consideration" referred to must have begun about the time Davis had shown his displeasure over what he considered Tinsley's negligence, in July, in connection with the loss of part of the fodder crop. Be that as it may, on the day the letter was received Davis made the following observation:

> This evening I received a note from Mr. Tinsley resigning his place as my overseer, after having deliberately Considered the matter for the last three months. I accept the resignation with Some regret, Since I desired that as we had borne the burden and heat of Summer, we might gather in Autumn the fruit of our labor. The task was light and the end of the year was at hand. Mr. T. expresses his reasons thus— 1 That my man Wash was competent to oversee my business & therefore I needed none other. I hope he Judges correctly of Wash's capacity—: I however preferred to have another & employed him. The second reason he assigns, places me under very great obligations for his candour & Sagacity—to wit that I am incompetent to attend to my duties by reason of my absent mindedness—I have heard it stated as the opinion of a great philosopher that all men are partially insane, and went on blundering through the world, for want of a friendly monitor to inform them of their lack of Sanity. I am more fortunate than Common mortals to be thus posted up on my true Condition & feel as grateful, as many others will feel astonished at the revelation—I really breathe

easier Since I have come to a knowledge of myself—& I shall escape Some of my errors & their consequences by getting this note of resignation—verily, verily—I believe So!

Two days later, as he had promised in his letter, Tinsley appeared at Beaver Bend to settle for his salary. As was usual when an over-seer quit before the end of the year for which he had contracted, he was given a note payable on the first day of the following January. Ten dollars having been advanced to him previously, he received a note for $272.00 for his services. Davis' reactions to this final meeting expresses his real feelings, and on the evening the settlement was made he stated:

. . . we parted friendly enough. I hereby declare that of all the men whom I have striven to render useful to me & to advance in business Success for himself I have made the greatest failure in him—Close & attentive to my business in most matter—giving me Satisfaction in governing my negroes & possessing more than ordinary quickness of perception—He & I failed to harmonize whenever we worked together—My plans never Suited him, nor did he ever Seem capable of what he was desired to do.

Two weeks after Tinsley left Beaver Bend another overseer by the name of Levi Harrison was located and began work with the under-standing that he should remain until Christmas, 1859, "if it is agree-able on both sides." Harrison turned out to be most acceptable, al-though in the spring of 1859 his work was held up by rainy weather with the result that through most of the year he was behind the usual schedule of operations at the plantation. On February 26, he lamented, "This has been the worse spring I ever saw for preparing a crop," and by March 12 he had planted only twenty acres of corn. In the previous year ninety acres had been planted by the same date. He had also bedded only two hundred acres of cotton land against two hundred and seventy in 1858. But as Davis admitted, "all planters are behind former years in preparation & planting," and Harrison was not cen-sured for slowness. The weather was excellent for work during the summer and autumn and by the first of December Harrison was able to report that he was about a month ahead of work completed the year before. On December 3, he added that "the weather up to the present has been fine for gathering cotton. It has been one of the best falls for gathering crops that I ever Saw." As a result, Harrison and his work was pleasing to Davis. During part of his tenure, moreover, he was in more complete authority than any overseer who had yet worked for Davis. On June 1, 1859, Davis had a paralytic stroke. From that date until November 22 he remained in his bed and even at the

latter date had to be carried bodily from his room in order to attend a
birthday dinner given in his honor. Because of his incapacitation,
his overseer was practically in absolute charge of affairs at Beaver
Bend. And, under Harrison's direction the plantation made the largest cotton crop in its history. He was of course rehired for the year
1860, but on February 25 of the latter year Davis made the following
entry in his farm book: "This day Mr. Harrison and I separated and
I paid him his wages—$83 to this Saturday night [his earlier salaries
having been paid] after he had lived with me 16 months. Mr. Harrison was a very obliging and kind hearted gentleman but in his plantation discipline he was too mild."

It comes as something of a surprise, considering Davis' physical
condition, that Harrison was not replaced with a white overseer.
Several men applied for the job, but rather than bring in a new person
Davis decided once more to act as his own superintendent and to turn
over actual supervision of plantation work to several of his slaves.
Such a move might not have been quite so unusual if Davis had possessed good health, but to allow his Negroes wide authority when he
could not personally check their work was an exceptional procedure
for a planter. His decision shows that he had complete confidence
in the ability of his slave leaders. Two days after Harrison departed,
Davis again appointed his Negro leader, Wash, to act as his chief
agent in the management of the plantation. Wash was placed in
general charge of business and, as in the previous period when Beaver
Bend had dispensed with a white overseer, Young Sol was named as
Wash's assistant. This time, however, another Negro named Johnson
was also appointed as assistant. The new set-up was as follows: Davis
issued orders to Wash, who was responsible for work done by the
various slave gangs. The gangs were under the direction of Young
Sol and Johnson. Wash checked on the gangs much in the same way
as an overseer, and reported each day to Davis on progress.

The season of the year when this new organization was initiated
is also of importance and shows definitely that Davis had great confidence in his Negroes. Moreover, on February 27, he stated that it
was a "very important time for the preparing of my corn land and
planting it. . . ." That he could not help in the work is shown by a
remark made on March 23, "My body is full of pain. My arm, my
side & leg are still stiff, sore & weak, too much for any action. I can

not walk or turn over in Bed without help." He was satisfied with his Negro leaders, however, and two weeks after their appointment he indicated that the hands were working exceptionally well under Wash's direction. But it seems that he had planned to hire an overseer to begin work as soon as his cotton lands were ready for planting on March 31. Still, he showed his satisfaction at this time with the work of his leaders by writing:

My plantation has been under Wash, Sol & Johnson as principal managers. The[y] have done much work and done it well. My plantation has improved 100 per cent in fences, roads, ditches and gates. The ploughing is very well done—the cutting down of canes, willows, and ditch banks has greatly improved my place. . . . My teams are improving—My Stock are doing well considering. . . . I have found that attention to my business is too laborious for my body and mind even while confined to my bed. Mr. John White agrees to come and attend to my business for some time and I hope he will find it agreeable to continue.

The new overseer, John White, was the best one Davis ever had at Beaver Bend. He was the son of Daniel O. White, one of Davis' best friends and neighbors, and had had experience on his father's plantation. He was hired particularly because Davis expected to be away from home for a few months. In order to obtain his temporary services it was necessary to pay him fifty dollars a month and furnish the use of a saddle horse. Always before Davis had underpaid his overseers. Now at last he paid a prevailing wage and for the first time he obtained a wholly dependable overseer. White was the best educated man to work for Davis. Of some significance, too, he was the only overseer who ever showed any interest in politics while at Beaver Bend. In this connection he wrote in the farm book, June 25, that a local newspaper "Speaks as if every person was crazy or nearly So about the nomination of Stephen A. Douglas by the Baltimore Convention for President. . . ." The next day, in referring to the excitement of the people in his region over Douglas' nomination, he added, "I think they better Save their ambition & animation both for the more laudable purpose of defeating him in his anticipation." Be this matter as it may, White agreed to work for Davis only because someone was needed to plant cotton, but even then agreed to stay on for only two or three months, or until the crop had been laid by.

As it happens, White continued with Davis until the end of September. While at Beaver Bend he had more complete control of affairs than any overseer between 1848 and 1862. One reason for this,

as it had been in the case of Levi Harrison, was Davis' illness, and
on the day he arrived he found his employer "complaining with the
most excrusiating pain." Moreover, during part of the time White
was at Beaver Bend, Davis was away from home having his ailment
treated. During that time White assumed complete supervision of the
plantation. Even before Davis left, however, the new overseer showed
himself to be a man after Davis' heart. From his arrival White worked
the Negroes harder than they had ever been worked before and made
them toe the line in every respect. On April 30, in describing the
condition of the plantation mules, he reported that the animals were
receiving "a good share of *Currycomb & Elbowgrease*" which he
thought to be "equal to half feed of corn any time." As a marginal
note to this entry in the farm book, Davis showed his approbation
with "Huza for Mr. White for Elbow Greece." White's close scrutiny
later in the year of the Negroes' job of picking cotton also indicates
his qualities as overseer. On August 4, he stated that his "first order
was to pick Cotton clear of leaves, dirt & trash of all kinds," continuing, "I expect to enforce the order and see that it is carried out to
the fullest extent as the Crop is biding fair to be Short. I want to
make it bring more money than the last years crop and that is the only
way to do it; the hands pick less in weight but more in reality than
last year." This and other evidences of his close attention to his employer's interests endeared him to the members of the Davis family.
When he left Beaver Bend, on September 30, it was recorded by Hugh
Davis, Jr., that "He left, carrying with him the gratitude & thanks
of our family for having sacrificed his pleasure to attend to Pa's business during his absence to the Virginia Springs."

Before leaving Beaver Bend White persuaded the elder Davis to
put his son, Hugh, Jr., who was seventeen years of age, in temporary
charge of the plantation. In the next month young Davis supervised
affairs at the place and did a very creditable job of directing the
Negroes while they were picking cotton, gathering pea and peanut
vines for fodder, cutting rice, digging ditches, and packing cotton
bales. But on November 1, Davis located a man by the name of
T. W. Porter who agreed to fill in as overseer. Porter worked all right
until Christmas, but two days afterwards he "packed up his things
& then went away to frolick & dance to spend the Christmas days."
Davis was put out at this; and on December 31 when Porter turned

up again and asked to be allowed to resume work he was dismissed because, as Davis graciously put it, the man "could not attend to so large a business with so little experience as he had."

The next overseer, the last one hired before the outbreak of the Civil War, was no better qualified. His name was A. P. Green and he worked at the plantation from January 3 until the first week of April, 1861. His education is shown by the following interesting note made on January 31 concerning the weather: "this Hes bin Desidly the Disagreeables month for Farm work that I ever witnesst. . . ." All of his entries in the farm book are just as quaint. In his period of service at the plantation he neglected his work by going every day or so to Hamburg or Marion to drill with a local military organization and to attend musters. His mind was not on his work, but rather on the expected war. His management of Beaver Bend naturally suffered and finally became so unsatisfactory that on March 4 Davis in desperation reminded him that he was not following orders and referred him to earlier farm books, with page numbers appended, containing all the rules that had been established at the plantation since 1848: "Get them by heart and repeat them as Scholars in Grammar. These rules are referred to in our contract & are the consideration looked to most watchfully by me & my eyes are prone to see . . . have no other rules in conflict—in them lies my pleasure and profit & I am in hopes your own too. All departures are Hazardous. Mr. Bates made a fortune by observing the maxim—'Obey orders, if you break owners.' His case Shows each will get rich. So can you & I." This appeal had no effect on Green, and on March 22 he was requested to read the statement which overseer White had made earlier concerning the use of "a good share of *Currycomb & Elbowgrease.*" Green was still unimpressed and within two weeks went off to war.

4

PURCHASE AND CARE OF SLAVES

ONE of the important responsibilities faced by Davis as owner and manager of Beaver Bend was the purchase and care of slaves. When he began his plantation activities he owned eighteen adult Negroes. Some had been acquired through purchases, several had been received in lieu of fees due him for legal services, others had come to him as gifts from his father, and others were acquired from his wife's relatives. At the time he owned an equal number of males and females, a ratio which he tried to maintain as long as he operated his plantation. This equality in numbers by sex does not mean, however, that all the grown slaves were married. Like other planters, Davis sometimes bought a man or woman regardless of their marital state, but there was no conscious effort on his part to separate families. Rather he keenly wished, whenever at all practical, to obtain the entire family of a particular Negro which he desired to purchase, that is, if the Negro were married. On occasions when entire families could not be bought he usually tried later to acquire the husband or wife of a slave he had obtained earlier. Such a practice was recognized as leading to more effective work on the part of the slaves and, of equal importance, resulted in a natural increase in the planter's number of slaves. But if Davis bought husbands and wives of his slaves especially to increase his holdings, he must have been disappointed because from 1848 through 1860 only sixteen Negroes were born at his place. Perhaps this was just as well from Davis' standpoint, for one of the most unprofitable aspects of plantation slavery was the care required of small Negro children. Care had to be provided, with little economic return, at least during their first ten years. The black children at Beaver Bend no doubt worked, but throughout the mass of Davis plantation records which have been examined only two references have been found in regard to jobs performed by the children. Then, they merely set fire to log heaps on one occasion and helped with the hoes in the other case. They must have performed other simple tasks, however, because it was the custom for slave children to help pick cotton, clean up plantation yards, and do other such jobs.

In one instance, early in his career at Beaver Bend, Davis made what he considered a financial sacrifice in order to purchase the wives of two of his Negro men. The purchases were made in 1852, and presumably were the first ones concluded after he took over his plantation. The incident is of interest, not only for the information concerning his desire to acquire the wives of men already owned, but also for the information it affords on prices being paid for slaves. Moreover, it indicates something of the usual trading practices followed by two typical blackbelt planters when they were bargaining over Negroes. In December, 1852, Davis was negotiating with Daniel O. White, another Perry County planter and father of John White referred to above, for the purchase of two females belonging to the latter. According to Davis, the preliminary dickering was described as follows: "Mr. White came to trade about the wives of my men— gave me his prices—Lucy—1000$. Eliza & her two children 1400. My price was 900 [for Lucy]—1200 [for Eliza and children]. I advanced to 2250 [for the four Negroes]—he receed to 2350. I refused & thus we parted—100$ apart." This trading, probably quite pleasant but in dead earnest on both sides, occurred on December 17. The next day, after more sparring, Davis recorded in his farm book that "Mr. White this evening recedes 50 Dollars on Eliza & I agree to take her— at 1300.00." A few days later, December 22, he wrote further about the deal, "Closed purchase of 4 slaves from Danl. O. White at $2300 —a hard bargain, but made necessary by circumstances, the women being the wives of my men—I feel Satisfied to have paid one hundred dollars Each more than they are worth; . . ." In the long run, however, these purchases turned out exceedingly well. Lucy soon showed herself to be the best cotton picker at Beaver Bend and from her arrival there consistently picked more cotton each year than any other man or woman on the place. Eliza was also a good buy. She took two boys with her when she went to Davis' plantation, and between 1852 and 1861 gave birth to three more boys and one girl. She was the most prolific woman Davis owned, and as long as slavery lasted she was considered an excellent possession. She also became the plantation cook, the most exacting and important job performed by a female on the place.

In January, 1853, immediately after the above purchases, Davis owned thirty-one slaves, his total holding having increased by eleven during his first five years as a planter. Fourteen of the Negroes were men, thirteen were women, and four were classed as children. A birth had occurred in 1848 and in 1850. Six were under ten years of age, three were between ten and fifteen, three between fifteen and twenty, eight between twenty and thirty, five between thirty and forty, three between forty and fifty, and two between fifty and sixty. The age of the thirty-first slave is unknown.

As might be expected, purchases of Negroes were continued as new land was cleared and put under cultivation. Some of the prices paid for slaves are demonstrated by the few records on the matter which are available. A Negro named Elect was bought for $1,225 on January 31, 1854. On December 31, 1855, after a visit to his father's plantation in Mississippi, Davis wrote in his farm book, "Started two wagons to Selma for my groceries & 4 negro boys I bought of my father at the prices following, viz Spotswood 21 years at 1250—Sam 19 at 1250—Hanover [no age given] at 1000—Moses 9 at 800—$4300— a very high price." The next year, on September 24, he "Bought 4 negro girls—Amy 16 [years old]—at 1100—Margaret 15 at 1050— Hester 13 at 950 & Eliza Anne [no age given] at 950—payee at 90 days from date." These females were paid for on January 9, 1857, when he signed drafts of $4,500 on his Mobile cotton factor. In these purchases of four "boys" in 1855 and four girls in 1856, Davis was again following his custom of maintaining an equal number of males and females at his plantation. Tom, a Negro man, was bought for $1,250, on January 1, 1857. On October 20 of the same year, $1,500 was paid for a woman named Adaline and her child. The method of paying for Adaline and her child was typical of many of the purchases

made by Southern planters. Davis held a note for $1,258.88 signed
by the man from whom the slaves were obtained. In putting through the
purchase he exchanged the note in his possession and gave his personal
note of $241.12 in payment of the woman and her offspring. No
money changed hands in the deal. The only other purchases of slaves
for which records exist occurred on March 6, 1858, when Davis
"brought some negroes" home from a trip to Memphis, Tennessee;
and on September 27, 1858, at which time two girls were obtained.
But he made many purchases, for the inventory of his estate shows
that he owned seventy-eight slaves at the time of his death in June,
1862. Only seven of the sixteen black children born at Beaver Bend
between 1848 and 1861 lived. The remaining sixty-seven slaves were
acquired, either before or after he began his career as a planter. The
final total of seventy-eight slaves owned very definitely places Davis
at the time of his death within the class of a large slave-owner. Furthermore, when his Negroes were appraised on January 12, 1863, they
were valued at $63,965.[1] It should be remembered, however, that this
was a war-time evaluation and that the figure by no means represents
the amount of money which had been invested.

At times it was necessary to augment temporarily the staff of Negroes at Beaver Bend. The need was usually solved by hiring a few
blacks, either for an entire year or for a shorter period during which
their services were especially required. When particularly hard pressed
for additional workers the overseer was put to the plow. On several
occasions the Davis boys worked in the field. Frequently those Negroes
who had a trade, which meant that they were customarily relieved of
work in the field, were forced to help out in an emergency. House
servants less often went out to work. Davis himself never toiled in
the field. Whenever Negroes were hired they were treated in the same
manner as those owned by Davis. An interesting point, too, is that in
one instance Davis employed two females because they happened to
be related to Negroes living at Beaver Bend. But being a practical,
hard-headed business man, he was not above using such a situation
to save on the amount of rent it was necessary to pay for the use of
the hired slaves. It is rather certain that his motive in this particular
case was for the most part a monetary one when he hired the two
women. On the other hand, the interest of the planter from whom

[1]Perry County, Alabama, Inventory of Estates, I, 928-935.

they were hired seems to have been in part a humane one. After some negotiations the planter, J. P. Graham of Perry County, wrote Davis, "I have concluded to accept your proposition, of $125 [a year] for the hire of Malinda & Mahala, although I could get more for them, but as you have the father of one & the brother of the other, & as they wish to be with them, I am willing to lose something to accommodate them . . . ." As will be shown, the price paid for the services of these Negroes was below the average.

The custom of hiring out Negroes had become well established in Alabama long before Davis became a planter. Davis himself had followed the practice before 1848, usually in order to pay off a debt. For example, in 1839, Davis hired out a Negro named Solomon at the rate of one dollar a day. The money received for Solomon's services was turned over to William Hornbuckle, a merchant of Marion with whom Davis had an account. Another use to which payments for hired Negroes was sometimes put is indicated by a case occurring in 1844. In that year Davis hired out two Negroes to H. F. Godden, of Marion, and Godden signed two promissory notes in payment of the services of the slaves. One note was, "By first of January, 1845 I promise Hugh Davis or order one hundred & twenty Dolls for Value received in the Services of Negro Woman in the year 1844 & also Promise to give Said negro woman the usual Winter & Summer Clothing." The second note for the use of the other slave was for one hundred dollars. Neither note was paid on time and on June 16, 1846, Davis assigned them to a man named Samuel Whitmen "for value received." It is impossible to say when the notes finally got back to Godden. So much at this point for the financial complexities of ante-bellum planters who conducted their business on a credit basis.

But enough of the digression. When Davis took over Beaver Bend in 1848 he was short-handed and had to hire two men for the year. The Negroes were hired from a planter named E. P. Perry and for them Davis paid $125 each, which was the usual rate being paid for a prime hand in the blackbelt. As was the custom, Davis also had to promise to furnish each hired hand with two summer suits, one winter suit, one hat, one blanket, two pairs of shoes, and to pay the taxes on him for the year in which the Negro was hired. It was expected that the hired hands should be in good health when they began their services, and Davis was required to return them in the same condition at

the end of the year. As was the custom, the slaves were to be returned
to their owner on Christmas Day of the year for which they had been
hired out. Although not the case in this particular transaction, sometimes an owner of the Negro being hired out demanded that the
planter or person using him also pay for any medical attention required while the hand was being used. On another occasion when
this condition was suggested Davis refused to pay a doctor bill for a
slave which he had hired.

As it happened, only in a few instances did Davis hire Negroes to
help with the work at Beaver Bend, his objection being that the practice was too expensive. The two men already mentioned were hired
during a rush season, that is, to help with laying by a cotton crop.
The two women referred to were hired because they could be obtained
cheaply, and in the summer of 1852 a man was hired to dig ditches
because none of Davis' slaves were yet proficient at the job. Between
1852 and 1861, only one Negro was hired. Therefore in a period of
fourteen years only six hired hands worked for Davis on his plantation,
and only one was engaged in the last ten years. The owner of Beaver
Bend expected his work to be done by his own hands, or perhaps hoped
that whenever he became short-handed he could borrow for a short
period Negroes belonging to his neighbors.

This custom of borrowing hands for a few days was in fact commonly practiced in the Alabama blackbelt, including Perry County.
Sometimes the slaves of neighbors worked together on such tasks as
constructing a fence or digging a ditch on the line dividing their plantations. The practice turned out admirably for the neighbors as long
as they were on good terms, but if one believed the other was en-
croaching on his land there was trouble. For example, while Davis
was a lawyer he tried to settle such a dispute between two planters
living near Greensboro, Alabama. His efforts failed and the argument
ended in a duel between the two men. Davis, however, never had any
such difficulties. Once while rolling logs in a field being cleared for
the plows he used his own field hands, nineteen of them, and "3 hands
besides my own. . . ." This was on April 7, 1854. On another occasion, when some of his Negroes were ill with typhus fever, a neighbor
sent several slaves to help pick the Beaver Bend cotton. A few years
later this courtesy was repaid when Davis allowed his own slaves to
plow and hoe cotton for the same neighbor, who "was sick—his hands

had measles—[and] 3 had been buried." This occurred on July 2, 1857, at a time of the year when it was necessary to continue work because it was the season for cleaning the cotton crop and the whole success of the crop depended on keeping hands in the fields. Davis furnished "9 plows & 21 hoes big & little." At another time, February 17, 1859, he exchanged the use of one of his Negroes for the use of one belonging to another neighbor, James T. Pack: "Mr. Packs Smith came today to work in Shop. Sent Harrison in his place." This custom of exchanging for a few days Negroes who had a trade was also a common practice in the region around Beaver Bend. Hired or exchanged slaves were treated in the same manner as those living on the plantation.

Although Davis rarely hired a Negro to work at his own plantation he had no aversion to hiring out his slaves to other planters. He seems to have looked on the practice as a means of making money. He even hired out a few of his Negroes for work on gangs used in the construction of railroads in Alabama during the 1850's, despite the fact that the work was considered the hardest and most gruelling a slave could do. More often, however, he merely hired out one of his well trained Negroes to a neighbor. One Beaver Bend slave name Wright seems always to have been on the go. An adept carpenter, he was one of the most expert and efficient slaves owned by Davis, and was always in great demand among the planters of Perry County. He was hired out during part of nearly every year from 1848 to 1862, in every case for twenty-five dollars a month, clothing, housing, and food. His services were desired so much that Davis always reserved the privilege of calling him home whenever he was needed there. It was always carefully stated, too, that Wright was never to be re-hired out. The Negro was the best purchase Davis ever made. Davis had bought Wright in May, 1847, for only $900, from his brother Stephen, who was a physician in Greensboro. Wright was bought on credit as was the usual case when Davis purchased a slave. Payment was made, in September, 1848, at which time a small legacy was received from a deceased member of the Davis family who had lived in Virginia.

In providing care for his slaves, hired hands and borrowed Negroes, Davis was faced with the usual demands on a planter. Of special importance was the attention which necessarily had to be given to housing facilities, food, clothing, and medical attention. The matter of the slave quarters was handled in the customary manner of the planters of the ante-bellum period. Slave cabins were constructed with logs which were obtained as land on the plantation was cleared. By January, 1851, there were eight cabins at Beaver Bend. All the unmarried men lived together in one group of buildings; the unmarried women had separate cabins, some distance from the men's quarters, for their own use. The remaining structures were used by married couples, with two couples living in each cabin. The unmarried men and women were quite crowded in their places. As new slaves were purchased, or the old ones married, additional cabins were constructed. Two were put together during the first three months of 1856. Four were under construction in November, 1858. Three more were begun in February, 1859. In the winter of 1859-1860, three others were completed. A final one was begun on November 1, 1860. If these were all the cabins in use at the outbreak of the Civil War, Davis was at that time employing twenty-three cabins to house his slaves.

Because of money invested in his slave property, if for no other reason, it was to Davis' advantage to attend carefully to the condition of the living quarters of his Negroes. He recognized fully the necessity of such care, and one of his plantation rules provided for the whitewashing, scouring, and cleaning up of the Negro cabins regularly. Special attention to slave quarters was required particularly in the late spring, summer, and early fall of each year. The slaves were forced to keep their places clean inside and outside, and their cabins were always subject to inspection either by Davis or his overseer. The usual custom of promoting better sanitation by frequently placing large quantities of lime under the cabins was followed. Smaller amounts were less often put under the beds of the Negroes. Although more lime was used for sanitation purposes during the summer months than at any other season of the year, there was actually no designated time for spreading it. It was put in place at the discretion of Davis or the overseer, or at the request of the slaves. They had the privilege of complaining if their living conditions became too unsatisfactory. Perhaps Davis was unusual in having floors and fireplaces constructed in all of his Negro cabins, thus insuring more comfort and better health conditions for his slaves. The floors, fireplaces and woodwork of the cabins were kept in good repair; and among the many jobs required of a group of slaves known as the "trash gang" was that of keeping the yard of the cabin lot cleaned of "Chips leaves & litter." At least once or twice a year, usually during the spring or summer months, the cabins were whitewashed. As Davis increased his knowledge of plantation management, he became more and more interested in providing good housing facilities for his Negroes. The appearance of the cabin lot received his special attention. The year 1860 serves as a typical case of his care in this respect. In the course of the year the entire cabin lot was cleaned off at least once a month. On December 24, in preparation for the Christmas holidays, the slaves were instructed to "clean up their houses & yards etc."

Another of Davis' major problems was that of furnishing food for his Negroes. Much of the food was produced on the plantation, but it was necessary to purchase some of it from commission merchants. Following the practice of the planters of his region and of the South, he supplied his hands with bacon sides and meal throughout the year. The two items comprised their main diet, although as might be expected there was a difference in the food with the change of seasons. During the winter of 1851-1852, for example, when Davis owned fourteen male and thirteen female hands, the group received one bushel of meal each day. In addition, each individual was rationed one-half pound of meat. Such was the winter diet. In the spring and early summer of 1852, the one bushel of meal for the group was continued. Meat for the individual was gradually decreased, but at no time completely cut off. By middle summer, both meal and meat had been cut in half because vegetables had been added to the diet. During the first two and a half years at Beaver Bend, Davis gave out Negro rations on Saturday afternoon of each week, but on July 6, 1850, he wrote in his farm book, "Directed change of time from Saturday to Monday for giving meal to the hands. Also to have the meal kept in the Smoke House & there measured." Davis was learning something of plantation management. His reason for such a change in the time of distribution was the Negroes' habit of gorging themselves on Saturday night and Sunday after receiving their rations. The result for them was a shortage of food before the next week-end. For Davis it meant complaints. His final solution of the problem was to appoint a plantation cook, and to ration out all food.

The Negroes' regular diet of meal, bacon and vegetables was sometimes supplemented with sweet potatoes, chicken and molasses, and on special occasions they were allowed to stuff themselves as much as they wished on the foods they loved most. This happened usually when some member of the Davis family celebrated a birth date, or at Christmas, or whenever a so-called summer or winter dinner was held. Their master began giving these annual dinners for his slaves early in his career as a planter, starting first with a summer dinner after the cotton crop had been laid by. The practice was continued until his death. His first reference to such an affair was made on July 29, 1850, when he recorded in his farm book that he "gave the negroes their Summer dinner." Such an occasion was a gala affair, and one to which the slaves looked forward with great anticipation. On July 3, 1852, there was a "Holiday Dinner—Barbecued lamb. Brunswick Stew." On April 20, 1853, it was recorded, "We have done a fine month's work— Holliday given to all hands, fished and frolicked— . . . had a May dinner in the grove— . . ." On July 28, 1855, one sheep, a kid and a goat were barbecued for the Negroes. That the Negroes enjoyed themselves on these occasions is shown by an overseer's statement, on July 10, 1858, that "The negroes had a fine dinner & enjoyed themselves finely." After another such celebration, on July 30, 1859, it was recorded that they "enjoyed it very much." Davis' own description of a summer dinner held on July 19, 1856, was as follows: "about 11 O K called off [the hands from work]—Swept around the cabins & the hands dressed for dinner—Our dinner consisted of the following Bill of Fare—Barbecue—1 mutton—1 kid & 1 Shoate—Boiled ham— Boiled Shoulder & cabbage—Soup Gumbo. Brunswick Stew—Corn etc. . . . The affair went off well, but the hands were Stopped a few minutes by a very pretty little Shower—& then resumed their places and did ample Justice to the Feast & after removing the Cloth we indulged in a treat of Watermelons & closed the evening with dancing & music to the tune of 'Cotton is King' all being merry & cheerful with a Crop quite clean."

Still another necessity of the Negroes which Davis had to provide was clothing. Here once more he followed the practices of the planters of his region. Every available source of information leads to the conclusion that he always furnished his slaves with ample clothing and that essential apparel was ordinarily issued twice each year. Summer outfits were given out either in April or June. Winter garments were distributed between October and January, the specific time depending upon the severity of the weather. Sometimes the winter clothes were given to the Negroes at Christmas time as a part of their Christmas gifts. The job of giving out clothes to the slaves was usually performed by the female members of the Davis family. There was no set rule about this, however, and on occasion Davis himself or his overseer distributed the clothes. A general idea of the kinds of clothes and something of the amount of each type issued to the Negroes at Beaver Bend between 1848 and 1861 may be gathered from the following chart:

CLOTHES ISSUED TO SLAVES AT BEAVER BEND, 1848-1861

Articles

Year	Pants	Shirts	Shoes	Coats	Hats	Blankets	Dresses	Caps	Bonnets	Socks	Chemises
1848	25	45	7	8	2	7	....	....	....	....	....
1849	....	....	....	....	....	....	....	....	....	....	....
1850	22	13	....	....	....	....	....	....	....	....	....
1851	36	17	....	8	....	5	8	....	....	....	11
1852	39	22	20	....	12	....	....	....	....	6	....
1853	....	....	16	....	12	6	....	....	....	....	....
1854	32	32	13	....	12	....	....	2	....	....	....
1855	44	26	28	....	....	....	....	....	....	....	....
1856	47	32	20	2	9	....	1	....	12	....	....
1857	19	....	....	3	....	9	....	....	....	....	....
1858	34	50	48	3	....	18	21	....	....	....	....
1859	....	....	....	....	....	....	....	....	....	....	....
1860	36	....	39	2	....	....	....	....	....	....	....
1861	54	10	25	....	....	....	41	....	....	....	35

This chart does not include all the clothes issued, but it does indicate most of them. It will be seen, too, that pants and shirts were considered as the most important items among Negro clothing. Ordinarily at any one time each Negro could expect for his own use at least two shirts, two pairs of pants, and one pair of shoes. These articles were issued nearly every year both to men and women. Hats, coats, blankets and other such durable articles were given out less frequently, but the records show that the Beaver Bend Negroes were comfortably dressed for the temperate weather which existed there.

Not only did Davis have to supply clothing, food and living quarters for his slaves, but as their owner he had to provide medical attention as well as these other more common necessities. It was to his interest as operator of Beaver Bend to maintain good health among his hands if he expected them to do good work and show him a profit from the management of his place. It was obvious that whenever a slave became ill another had to take over his job, some one had to be hired to perform his work, or the work had to be postponed. Accordingly in order better to assure healthful conditions and to operate Beaver Bend more effectively, Davis followed several precautionary practices by which he hoped to prevent diseases among his Negroes. Prepared medicines consisting of arrowroot, of asafoetida, and of a mixture of arrowroot and camphor were bought for his slaves shortly before taking over direction of Beaver Bend. In 1848, a dentist examined the teeth of several of the Negroes. In the summer of 1852, after an epidemic of fever which had caused the death of three of his slaves, Davis purchased apothecary weights and ten dollars worth of quinine and dosed all his hands. Quinine was usually given on the slightest provocation. Another practice was to have the Negroes wash off regularly in the river, and frequently to wash and scrub their bodies, clothes, cabins, and bedding. Also during cold weather huge quantities of wood were hauled to the Negro cabins in order that the slaves might keep themselves warm and thus partially prevent such ailments as common colds, influenza, and pneumonia. In April, 1857, when an unseasonal, heavy snow came, Davis recorded, "I had to haul wood for the cabins today as a matter of humanity to the negroes— I am afraid of Pneumonia among them."

At another time Davis stated that he had established a "quarantine to prevent the Spread & catching of the Scarlet fever. My people are forbidden to go to preaching." Again, he described his precautions as follows: "The weather has become very wet & the health of the family is likely to change for the worse—we must use every caution— fire—dry feet at night—clean clothes & houses—in a word comfort for all is the Safety of all." On another occasion when a few of the slaves had fevers, he gave the sick ones and all others large doses of quinine regularly and thus prevented a spread of the ailment. In 1857, shortly after two Negro children died of whooping cough, he began inoculating his Negroes to guard against future attacks. Still another precaution, begun in 1858, was to weigh his Negroes from year to year in order to check partially on their health. Almanacs were commonly used by Davis and other blackbelt planters as a means of speculating on unhealthy seasons of the year and helped somewhat in determining the precautions which should be taken against diseases. As evidence of this custom, a physician friend of Davis wrote to a dispensery in 1851, "I have calls daily for your Almanacks as there is none in our reach. . . . I hope you wont fail to Send me a lot of Almanacks, as they are much Kneeded."

In most cases when the Negroes were treated for diseases and ailments they were given medicines which had been made at Beaver Bend. The medicine was also usually administered either by Davis himself or by his overseer. One of the chief requirements of the overseer was the ability to recognize and treat simple ailments and diseases. To be sure, some trained doctors practiced in the Alabama blackbelt, but in many instances they seemed to know no more than enlightened planters and quite frequently prescribed treatments already being employed by slave-owners. As a consequence Davis and many of his planter acquaintances most often relied on their own initiative when a Negro had a minor ailment, and at times even when a major disease became evident. Their homemade cures were widely used and knowledge of them was spread throughout the blackbelt by publication in many farm journals, newspapers, and almanacs which found their way into the parlors of most planters.

The cures employed called for much imagination, plus a great amount of experimentation and fortitude. Here was empiricism at its best. Barks and roots of trees, plants and herbs of all kinds were used in the concoction of homemade medicine. At times some planters cultivated in their gardens special plants which were believed to have great medicinal powers. Iron, whiskey, wines and any other article suspected of possessing healing qualities were commonly used in this domestic manufacture of medicines. It is significant, too, that use of such materials in the treatment of Negroes and whites was not confined to the Alabama blackbelt. There is evidence to show that such practices were in many cases followed throughout the eastern section of the United States during the ante-bellum period.[2] As people went

[2] Weymouth T. Jordan (ed.), "Martin Marshall's Book; Introduction," *The Alabama Historical Quarterly*, II (Summer Issue, 1940), 158-168; and the same editor's "Martin Marshall Book: Herb Medicine," *ibid.*, II (Winter Issue, 1940), 443-459; "Martin Marshall's Book: Homemade Medicine," *ibid.*, III (Spring Issue, 1941), 117-129; and "Martin Marshall's Book: "Farming and Veterinary Practices," *ibid.*, III (Summer

West they of course carried their customs along. Empiricism was country wide.

Throughout his activities at Beaver Bend, Davis also employed regular practitioners to attend to his slaves, and a physician was always called in whenever a valuable Negro became ill and also whenever any illness among the blacks seemed serious. Doctors were usually in attendance, too, when a Negro child was born at the plantation. One case of a physician's visit to attend a slave was described by Davis on January 20, 1856, as follows:

Ewell has this week exhibited Some weakness of mind, great aversion to labor, drowsiness—enormous appetite, having a clean tongue & very fine healthy evacuations—regular pulse at 85 to 88—I incline to think his mental powers impaired—Cause unknown— . . . examined by Dr. Jones, who gives it as his opinion, that the mind is affected only from Sympathy with the body—that he has eaten too much—at Some one time over loaded his Stomach, perhaps had a fit unseen—He prescribes (of course) Calomel & afterwards Oil & Turpentine—to be followed with Small doses of Turpentine every other day taken in Slip[pery] Elm Mucilage.

At another time a Negro woman had typhoid fever and was visited every day by a doctor. Sometimes the doctors brought good results; at other times they brought only criticism. This last outcome is borne out by the following observation made by a Beaver Bend overseer, on June 12, 1859, after a Negro had died because of what was considered the negligence of the doctors in attendance: a thorn had caused a slave's foot "to mortify—he was the worse treated by the physicians of any body I ever saw by way of not caring if he did die—they were Messrs. Jackson and McCain."

Because of the location of Beaver Bend along the banks of the Cahaba River Davis was often troubled with fever among his family and his Negroes. The fever, probably the disease which is today known as malaria, was present every year; and among the planters of the blackbelt there was always the fear of an epidemic coming to their region from the southern counties of Alabama. One method of handling the malady and of attempting to prevent its spread is described in a letter, of an unknown date, which Davis received from a friend and neighbor, James T. Pack, who was absent on a visit. In his letter he requested that Davis look after the Pack slaves in case any other Negroes in the neighborhood contracted fevers. In such case, Davis

Issue, 1941), 248-261. For a more general account, see Martha Carolyn Mitchell, "Health and the Medical Profession in the Lower South, 1845-1860," *Journal of Southern History*, X (November, 1944), 424-446.

was directed to have Pack's overseer go with all his slaves "off Some where in the Pine land. . . ." If any one of Pack's slaves got the fever, an old Negro woman named Nancy was to stay at home to nurse him, and Davis was asked to send "for the best Phisician or Phisicians and run the others off in the hills. . . ." This practice of taking Negroes to uplands in time of epidemics was widely followed. There is no record, however, of Davis following the custom at Beaver Bend. But on October 6, 1851, after six of his Negroes were put to bed in a typhus fever epidemic, two having died of the disease, he did move the rest of his hands to the nearby plantation of his brother-in-law, Osmond T. Jones.

When the Davis slaves got an ordinary fever they could expect one of several treatments. One was to take so-called blue mass pills. Sometimes they were given a dose of medicine known as No. 6, which their owner made from one pound of gum myrrh, two ounces of cayenne pepper, and one gallon of alcohol or French brandy. The most elaborate prescription for the disease consisted of a three-day treatment. On the first day the slave with the fever was given doses of blue mass, castor oil, pleurisy root tea and poultice and quinine; the next day came calomel, more castor oil and a dose of spirits of turpentine; on the third day he was supposed to be free of fever, but his ordeal was climaxed with quinine, butterfly root tea, chicken soup, and rice. A more simple treatment for fever was to administer calomel and castor oil the first day the ailment became noticeable and follow the next day with butterfly tea to produce perspiration and with a big dose of quinine.

Only a few other prescriptions have been located which Davis used in doctoring his Negroes at various times while he operated Beaver Bend. Many Alabama and Southern cotton planters kept a so-called plantation medical journal in which they recorded cures for the many diseases and ailments which prevailed in the region. If Davis kept such a book it has been misplaced. His farm books contain enough cures, however, to indicate that he followed the same practices in medicine as his contemporaries. For cholera morbus among his slaves he used mustard, camphor, elim water and calomel; for dysentery, the most common ailment of Negroes of the Deep South unless it were fever, he gave blue mass pills and laudanum and rubbed laudanum on the stomach; for swelled feet and legs, iron, elder tea and quinine; for snake bite, whiskey; for influenza, blue mass, castor oil and pleurisy root tea; for common bad cold, mustard plaster, rubbing with turpentine, pleurisy root tea and lobelia; and for ingorgement of the womb, calomel, rhubarb, a warm bath three times a day and an enema of warm water and laudanum. On April 18, 1855, a Negro sick with influenza was "doing well on the let alone treatment." These are the only cures of Davis' which are available. All of them except the last one were his own; the last one was recommended by a physician.

In order to maintain a record of the number of days which his slaves lost from work because of illness Davis had his overseer keep a "Sick List" each year. Part of the "Sick List for 1849" is reproduced here:

Jan.   9   Ann lost ten days with the measels
Jan. 10   Dick broke out with the measels and lost ten days and the same time George
           was sick and lost six days
Jan. 20   Arch and Lizabeth broke out and lost each ten days with measels
Jan. 31   George broke out with the measels and lost ten days
Jan. 24   Rachel lost five days on account of Sickness
Feb. 12   Jo was taken with the measels and lost ten days
Mar.   9   George left for the woods & returned the 14th Inst.
Mar. 13   Martha was Snake bitten the 5 March & went to work 13th—loss of 7 days.
May   25   Ann was sick and lost six days and Archer lost four days
Jun. 14   Rachel taken sick, & lost 4 days
Jun. 25   Solomon was taken sick; & lost 4 days—Wash lost two days with Chills
July   9   Rachel was taken sick and lost 8 days and Solomon lost 15 days
July 12   Ann was taken Sick. And died 28th July

This chart is quite indicative of health conditions among the Negroes at Beaver Bend, but it does not show one condition: namely, that fever and dysentery were the most common ailments among them. Moreover, other maladies with which Davis had to contend were influenza, ague, whooping cough, sore eyes, typhus fever, spasms, sore toe, grippe, eruption of the skin, spider bites, sore backs, dropsy, sore feet, bilious fever, headaches, broken bones, and laziness. These were the sicknesses most frequently mentioned by Davis and his overseers. Six Negroes died at the plantation between 1848 and 1861 and during that period, as far as can be ascertained, there were seventy-four cases of illness among the slaves. Nine hundred and eleven days were lost from work as a result of the cases. Thus, on the average, some Beaver Bend Negro was absent from work because of illness about every fifth day. Perhaps it should be pointed out that the above chart or "Sick

List for 1849" is not representative in that during the months covered by it there was an epidemic of measles at the plantation.

One other matter should be mentioned before bringing to a close this discussion on medical attention rendered to the Davis Negroes. It is that they often pretended to be ill in order to be excused from their work. It is worthy of note also that they rarely used such an excuse while Davis was present at the plantation, but usually on those occasions when he was away on a pleasure or business trip. Because of this habit of theirs the slaves at times received very little consideration from the overseer who had been left in charge during their master's absence. Once when a Negro came in from the field complaining of a headache, he was given a large dose of castor oil and sent back to the field. Again, a slave named Old Sol, who will be mentioned later in regard to his other misdeeds, was laid up with what he claimed to be a pain in the hip. When it was remembered that he had the same pain every year about the same time, he was given a big dose of medicine and put to shelling corn. On another occasion when Davis was away, in the summer of 1858, five Negroes suddenly became ill and did no work during their owner's absence. That they consciously neglected their work is shown by the fact that they laid themselves up from such maladies as drinking too much water, stone bruises, and overeating.

It was because of such occurrences as the above, as well as the necessity of supervising the Negroes in all their activities, that Davis believed, along with all planters, that it was essential to establish specific rules for the control and management of his slaves. That such was the case, however, does not lead to the conclusion that any large number of the Beaver Bend Negroes were negligent. Under ordinary circumstances they were hard-working, competent, and obedient. The rules set up for their control, the manner in which they performed their work, the methods practiced by Davis in order to keep them satisfied, and other aspects of their existence at Beaver Bend form a most interesting chapter in the study of the conditions under which they lived. Discussions of these phases of Negro life on Davis' plantation form the basis of the next part of this account.

5

MANAGEMENT AND WORK OF SLAVES

F ROM the examination made of various sets of rules which Davis worked out and evolved for the conduct of his slaves, it seems that his attitude toward his Negroes, as well as his conception of his own responsibilities toward them, was typical of the more enlightened group of ante-bellum planters living in and near the Alabama blackbelt. Included in his first entry in his 1848 farm book was a list of rules which he expected his hands to obey while they lived and worked at Beaver Bend. The specific acts which his Negroes were forbidden to commit, in the order in which they were enumerated in the rules, were: No Negro could stop his work and go to his cabin without first reporting and receiving permission from the overseer; a slave could not leave the plantation under any circumstance "without permission at any time, even when starting to see his wife" (this rule perhaps was not strictly enforced, for on May 4, 1856, Davis wrote in his farm book, "My negroes to wit: Wash George and Old Sol call for permits to go to Mr. Rose's—this is granted for today—But is positively to be refused to one and all hereafter"); the Negro could not feed his own chickens out of the plantation corn crib; he was never to sell fruit, nor gather it for eating purposes unless he received special permission from the overseer; he should never enter the nearby Cahaba River unless the overseer were present to watch over him (despite this rule, a Negro drowned in the river on June 4, 1853. The incident was described by the overseer as follows: "This evening the men was all in the river bathing and Ralph drowned him selfe—which was hurtful to all and much loss to the imployer—the caracter of this boy was prudent and true to his businis.") ; during the summer months the slave was allowed two hours intermission from field work, one hour being used to eat and to rest, the other hour to feed, curry, rub and wash the teams; and, lastly, the slave was to keep all fences and rails in place. If a Negro broke any of these rules, Davis decreed that the wrong-doer was "to be censured for the first time" and that for the second offense he was to be "punished with Stripes" by the overseer. One of the "GENERAL RULES & DIRECTIONS EVERY YEAR," which have been already mentioned, concerned the Negro. It was, "And those Servants which know the Stewards well and the masters rules and do not according thereto, Shall be beaten with many Stripes. But he that knew them not Shall receive few Stripes." In such manner the master of Beaver Bend admonished his slaves to know the rules and behave themselves and prevent their receiving even a "few Stripes."

In January, 1851, after three years of operating his plantation, but before moving out there from Marion, Davis saw fit to elaborate slightly upon the regulation for the conduct of his slaves. According to the new rules, no Negro was to have any authority over another and it was required specifically that a slave was never to "use the whip at all." The slaves could not trade, buy or sell with Negroes off the plantation, except by their master's or the overseer's written orders mentioning precisely the articles to be purchased or sold. If a Beaver Bend slave were found guilty of disobeying this order, he had to forfeit his share of the cotton crop made during the year the violation occurred; this was for the first offense; for the second he was to be punished. Finally, it was ordered that no Negro was to be considered sick until he reported his illness, and if he believed himself to be ill he was required to report immediately to the overseer. Directions to the overseer for treatment of a Negro when he reported himself ill was, "first give him a Sobelia puke, 3 times in 24 hours—if he refuses or neglects to take the medicine, give 39 lashes & Send him back to [the] field, unless the fever is very high, in which case Send for me. A Sobile puke is prepared—2 tea Spoons of Sobelia in a pint & a half pitcher—2 teaspoons of Composition & two of Nervene in another pitcher. Put in each a pint & half of hot water. Mix & Stir & then Stand half an hour—Dose ½ tea cup full every 15 minutes, till copious puking. The nervene in the Sobelia is Said to be best."

After the 1851 rules were established it was ten years before Davis again announced any further specific rules for the control of his Negroes, and then the regulations were included in a list of directions which were worked out at the time especially for a new overseer. These rules, of January 3, 1861, concerned the slaves as much as the overseer, however. They are self-explanatory:

1. The first duty of the overseer is to blow a horn or ring a bell at day light for all hands to rise and prepare for work as early as there is sufficient light.

2. As soon as feeding is done the overseer is expected to repair to the several places of work to overtake stragglers if any, and see that they start for a good days work; he is expected to see all provision troughs & have them kept well cleaned.

3. He is expected always to keep the water trough quite full when the drawers leave it every evening.

4. Men alone are required to feed and perform all lot work at the close of every day. The women are required when work is done in the field to sweep their houses and yards and receive their supper at the call of the cook, after which they may sew or knit but not leave their houses otherwise.

5. On corn shelling night the women shuck the corn and carry away the shucks to the cows, all helping together.

6. Supper is to be carried by cook and food carriers and left at their [the slaves'] houses at breakfast and dinner and no one is to be at the cook shelter except cook and carriers and each hand is to furnish his own vessels.

7. At 9 o'clock horn blows which calls every one to his place of rest at night and farther travelling out of doors and all communication between house servants and those at the cabins strictly forbidden after that hour.

8. All washing and mending done at the quarters for plantation hands.

These rules and those of 1848 and 1851 were the only specified ones under which the Negroes worked and lived at Beaver Bend throughout most of the period during which Davis owned and operated his plantation. It seems evident, however, that other rules and regulations were added from time to time. Such a probability seems even more likely after examining the many items concerning activities of slaves mentioned in the Davis papers and farm books, even though no rules as such were designated during the period from 1848 to 1861.

Furthermore, Davis set up his very elaborate and extended group of rules in June, 1862. These rules, his last ones, were of course written down after the opening of the Civil War, but it is impossible to determine to what extent they were the result of changed conditions brought on by the War. It is more probable that the 1862 rules were enforced long before they were formally established for the simple reason that it is extremely unlikely that such an all-inclusive collection of regulations could have been decided upon on short notice. Indeed, as has been mentioned in another connection, such detailed directions for managing Beaver Bend as those of 1862 could have resulted only from long experience as a planter and manager of slaves. Moreover, it should be further observed that the 1862 rules not only represent lessons Davis had learned from his own experiences, but also that they included ideas and practices resulting from observation of methods followed by his friends and neighbors. Obviously, too, some of the rules resulted from his examination of articles in the leading newspapers and periodicals of his period. In addition, the rules may be considered as part of his legacy to his sons. His voluminous papers nowhere indicate that he expected the South to lose the war in which it was involved. President Lincoln's Emancipation Proclamation had not yet been issued, and it was confidently expected that slavery would continue. Similar to most other planters of his type he thought that his sons would continue to operate a plantation with slave labor after the conclusion of the war. Thus, in recording his last rules, on June 1, 1862, he was merely passing on to his sons what he considered to be worthwhile knowledge gained from more than fourteen years experience in the successful management of his slaves and Beaver Bend.

Included in the rules of 1862 were directions for the daily supervision of the general activities of the slaves. An ordinary day's work of the slaves was therein partially outlined; and again it is assumed that the work outlined was typical of a day at Beaver Bend before 1862. After rising at day light and feeding the plantation animals under the direction of the overseer, the Negroes went to their respective places of work. No straggling was allowed, and the slaves began "a good day's work." As supervisors of the various tasks of the day, especially hoeing and plowing, Negro leaders were named for each of the several squads which were performing particular jobs. Wash and Young Sol were the chief leaders. They and others appeared before the overseer's house each night to report on the day's work. Each leader gave an account also of "the conduct of all under him—and . . . [was] responsible for the truth and accuracy of his reports." He then received orders for the tasks to be done the next day. The plantation cook prepared all food for herself, the slaves and the overseer, unless the latter happened to be married and his wife were present at the plantation. All the bread corn which the cook used had to be ground at the plantation mill and carefully weighed and measured. Her chief duties were to have breakfast ready to be distributed within an hour after sun-up, dinner at twelve o'clock noon, and supper before sundown. An important rule provided that the meals should be "at all times quickly shared out to the different hands and delivered to the food carriers" and that the cook assist with the distribution of food whenever necessary. Both breakfast and the noon meal were carried to the hands at the places where they happened to be working. Supper was delivered to the cabins of the various Negro families or to the cabins of the unmarried males and females. In order to prevent an unequal distribution of food and to save on costs of food, it was ruled emphatically that "no hand, man or woman, is to stay at the cook shelter except the cook and suckling women engaged with their babies." After supper the slaves had to go to their cabins and remain there. When the overseer blew his horn at nine o'clock they were expected to retire. Soon afterwards the overseer made his round of the cabins and called the roll to check on the presence of the slaves. If one failed to answer when his name was called he was later punished with twenty stripes.

Special rules for the slave women were also established, although in some respects they did not differ from the rules of 1861. Females were not allowed to perform the feeding of animals or to do any of the other so-called "lot work" in the late afternoons. Men only could attend to these tasks. It was reiterated that when the women finished their field work for the day they should go immediately to their houses "and engage in sweeping, fetching water for their families, receiving their suppers from the meal carriers to be sent by the cook—after which they may sew, knit or patch but in no event to leave their houses or go visiting." On corn shelling nights they assisted in shucking the corn, and carried the shucks to the cow house. A suckling woman was considered as half a hand, was given three quarters of an hour extra time each day to attend to the feeding of her child, and was never allowed to work more than half a mile from her cabin in order that she might hurry home in case her child needed her care. Any case of adultery which might occur should be strictly punished, and under the heading of "IMMORALITY" it was ruled that "All cursing, quarrelling, fighting and all violations of the right of husband and wife and such other immorality will meet with chastisement. From 10 to 50 stripes is the general measure of punishment for stated offenses according to their grade." This punishment of fifty stripes, probably for adultery, is the most severe mentioned at any point in the materials used in this study.[1]

In addition, the slaves were punished for two other specified failings, namely: twenty stripes for "falling to sleep in the open air or any out house;" and a "damage penalty from 10 to 39 stripes" for failure to report damages occurring to plantation equipment immediately after the mishap. This last punishment applied especially to wagoners and plowmen. When chastised for these or any other infractions of the rules, Davis decreed that the whipping be inflicted with "a broad leather flail or strap and not by whips, switches, cowhides" and that "all punishment should be administered for the purpose of humane discipline and free from passion." As a further indication of his humaneness toward his slaves he concluded his rules with a provision which he designated as "PROTECTION TO NEGROES," "Fully acknowledging responsibilities of the Masters not only for wholesome discipline but a merciful protection to those whom the laws of God and man have placed under his, my charge; it is allowed and can not be denied, and would not be denied except for purposes of cruelty and deception, that each and every slave shall communicate to the master all things proper to be known, in the masters judgment, especially such as have reference to his food and its supply, his clothing, or the deficiency thereof, his punishment, the quantity an[d] cause thereof, the existence of any known immorality and the parties engaged in it etc.—he [said slave] being responsible for any false communication according to the Masters judgment."

It is well at this point, now that the development of Davis' rules for the conduct of his slaves has been discussed, to turn to a consideration of the execution of some of those rules. It should be stated

---

[1]Such a ruling partially refutes the general claim of certain abolitionists of the antebellum period that licentiousness was openly practiced on every plantation operated in the South. A. Y. Lloyd, *The Slavery Controversy* (Chapel Hill, 1939), pp. 49-101, has an excellent summary of the charges made by abolitionists against Southern planters in the period before the Civil War.

first, however, that as far as can be ascertained, the owner of Beaver Bend was always just and lenient toward his Negroes in carrying out his disciplinary measures. No record is available to show that the elder Davis was ever harsh in the management and treatment of his slaves. On the other hand, he had the reputation of being particularly kind toward them. Perhaps he was too kind according to the standards of some of his friends and fellow Perry County planters. There is no evidence that he ever whipped a Negro, but it is known that he always insisted that his overseers execute his rules and punish the Negroes for any disobedience. On several occasions he even went so far as to dismiss overseers who were too lenient or who failed to perform satisfactorily this part of their work. But as it happened, the overseers were not often compelled to punish the blacks, because they were usually well behaved. Still the fact that punishment was meted out whenever believed to be necessary shows that Davis was similar to other planters of his region. Most planters believed that under certain circumstances in handling Negroes nothing would take the place of a sound whipping. Since Davis owned seventy-eight slaves at one time he was bound to have problems of discipline. The peculiar institution being what it was it would have been quite unusual to bring together seventy-eight Negroes who would always obey orders and accept philosophically their position of human bondage. At Beaver Bend they were whipped, although not with the same severity, as they were whipped at most plantations of the ante-bellum South.

As was the case with most planters, at times Davis had the problem of runaway slaves. In most instances, however, the Negroes did not leave Beaver Bend with any intention of remaining away permanently. They usually left merely to get a little taste of freedom for a day or so, or took to the woods to spend a night or perhaps a few days. From 1848 until 1861, runaways occurred fifteen times, and such a total seems small for a planter who owned as many slaves as Davis. It is of noteworthy importance, too, that most of the runaways occurred in the late ante-bellum period. Two Negroes left on two occasions each before the end of 1855. A total of eight slaves left the plantation on five occasions in 1858 and afterwards, three of them leaving twice. There seems to be little doubt that this increase in the number of runaways in the late years before the Civil War was brought about by the growing political and social pains developing in the South as a result of the Abolition Crusade. It is quite probable that some of the Beaver Bend slaves were approached by persons sympathetic to the principles of abolitionism. Be that as it may, the whole problem of runaways was never a major one with Davis.

The most consistent trouble-maker among the Beaver Bend slaves was an elderly Negro named Old Sol. He should perhaps be pitied more than censured, however. His faults were numerous and petty, although he ran away twice during a period of twelve years. Then he merely took to the woods for a day or so. Another slave twice left the place on Sundays, but again only to enjoy a little temporary freedom. At another time an overseer reported, after Davis had returned from a short trip, that a Negro had "taken French leave of absence this morning." Again, three slaves "left for parts unknown." Davis wrote in his farm book, on May 20, 1859, that "Harrison & Hester ran away to get married—I wish them a pleasant bridal tour & Speedy & Safe return to their friends who will no doubt give them a warm reception." The couple was caught by a patrol at Cahaba and placed in jail and kept there for two days. As was the custom when slaves ran away and were caught, on this occasion their owner was notified. Davis did not seem to be especially surprised when the Negroes were brought back to Beaver Bend; and his chief concern seems to have been the twenty dollars he had to pay for their return. He described the payment of the sum, which was a sort of reward as well as payment for the board and room and transportation of the runaways, as "A pretty tough." It may be confidently assumed that he provided Harrison and Hester with a whipping as a wedding present. Later, on April 9, 1860, an overseer caught a Negro named May "playing truant and paid him down cash." Six days later it was reported that another slave "went off without permission for which I will Settle tomorrow."

The complacency with which Davis and his overseers accepted these runaways is not at all surprising. Alabama was a long way from free territory, and a runaway from the blackbelt had to run the gauntlet of patrol systems in several states. To get out free was hard indeed. The blackbelt planters were justly confident that the patrol system of apprehending runaway slaves would usually bring them back. In Perry County, as elsewhere in Alabama, every planter who was physically fit served patrol duty. About once a month Davis and a group of his neighbors served their term on a patrol and went about the countryside beating bushes in much the same manner as when hunting opossums. The accompanying shouting, gun-shooting and barking of dogs must have frightened the wits out of any slave who might have worked up enough courage to run away from home.

Stealing by the Negroes was another perceptible habit with which most plantation and slave owners had to contend.[2] Beaver Bend Negroes were no different than others, but here again, however, Davis was fortunate, or perhaps he was able to control his Negroes so well that they refrained from the practice. Maybe they were more honest than others, maybe they stole with more finesse than others. Anyhow, the records of activities at the plantation contain relatively few references to thefts by the slaves. As far as is known, the first case of stealing occurred on May 29, 1855, more than eight years after Davis took over his plantation. An entry was made in the farm book concerning a Negro who had taken some corn to a nearby mill to be ground into meal: "George brought back 1073 [pounds]—or 62 lbs. too much meal—before he was 53 [pounds] too little—This is the clearest proof of Rascality." What punishment George received for his naive effort to fool his master was never recorded, but it is rather certain that some sort of chastisement resulted. This practice of the slaves stealing corn on the way to mills near Beaver Bend became so prevalent that Davis finally constructed a mill of his own, both to save on the cost of grinding corn and to prevent petty pilfering by his Negroes.

A rather unusual settlement of the case of another kind of theft occurred at Beaver Bend on October 10, 1855. Old Sol was the culprit. He was caught stealing cotton, but his master let him off on bond, so to speak. Davis described the settlement of the case as follows: "Daniel, Wright, Pompey, & Ewell [four of the best Negroes on the plantation] Stand for Old Sol & bargain to take 39 lashes each in case he is again caught Stealing on the place & by this Old Sol gets clear of 39 [lashes] for Stealing Cotton out of the gin." The final

[2]General information on various aspects of slavery may be found in Davis, *The Cotton Kingdom in Alabama*; W. Brewer, *Alabama: Her History, Resources, War Record, and Public Men* (Montgomery, 1872); Ulrich B. Phillips, *American Negro Slavery* (New York, 1918); William E. Dodd, *The Cotton Kingdom* (New Haven, 1919); Charles S. Sydnor, *Slavery in Mississippi* (New York, 1933); Ralph B. Flanders, *Plantation Slavery in Georgia* (Chapel Hill, 1933); and Winston J. Coleman, Jr., *Slavery Times in Kentucky* (Chapel Hill, 1940).

outcome of Old Sol's thieving activities is unknown, but it was not long before his good intentions, if he had any, were overcome by his bad habits. On August 4, 1857, there was recorded in the farm book, "Old Sol confessed his theft—a Sheep." The old man must have been a victim of kleptomania. Certainly he was not hungry. Whether he alone, or his four bondmen received punishment was not recorded.

At least on one occasion a Negro was punished for failure to follow Davis' rule that the slaves should "perform the work well under the overseer." John White, who began overseeing at Beaver Bend on April 1, 1860, "had to whip Sophronia for not sowing [cotton] seed as directed." This occurred four days after White arrived at the plantation. Later he had to punish two women for fighting. There is no way of determining the reactions of the Negroes in most cases of beatings, but being human beings they naturally resented receiving a whipping. As far as can be ascertained, however, only on two occasions did a slave object openly to physical punishment. One such incident occurred on February 18, 1858, when an overseer started to punish a woman for her carelessness in breaking four plough stocks within one week. The woman grabbed an axe and brandished it in the face of the overseer. She refused to be whipped, but when the overseer struck at her with his cane she dropped the axe and ran. Reconsidering, she returned to the overseer and took her beating. At the time Davis was away from the plantation and as described by the overseer, "I gave her a good whipping and intend to give her another when Mr. Davis returns." The other incident is that of a Negro flying into a rage because of what he considered harsh treatment. The man had been serving as Davis' coachman, a most desirable job, but for some reason was dismissed from his sinecure and sent to the fields as a common field hand. In revenge for this face-losing demotion, the slave set fire to one of the plantation barns, and Davis estimated later that the Negro's fit of temper resulted in a loss of property amounting to $750. A few days later the man was taken to Selma and placed on board a river boat bound for Mobile, "to be Sold in a far off land." This occurred on March 19, 1857. That the Negro was indeed incorrigible is shown by his activities after leaving Beaver Bend. He was sold in Mobile, hired out to a railroad construction gang, ran away from his job, was caught, and punished. These two cases of punishment at Beaver Bend are exceptions. Notwithstanding them, there is a paucity of available material on which to base any definite conclusion concerning the actual amount of physical punishment received by the Beaver Bend slaves. On the whole, few references were made to the subject in the records kept by Davis. Perhaps in some cases his omissions were intentional, but all the evidence seems to indicate that few punishments were necessary at his plantation.

It is very probable that one reason Davis had so little trouble in managing his slaves was his own strict adherence to the rules which he established. He followed the rules as closely as he expected all others to follow them. He demanded that the Negroes perform the work outlined for them in the regulations, but at the same time he also recognized the privileges which were granted to them. For example, in keeping with his orders concerning night and Sunday work, whenever a Negro did extra work he was usually rewarded. There were exceptions to this of course. One occurred on Sunday, March 23, 1856, when he worked his slaves without pay because the work of the plantation was behind schedule and the cotton was grassy. At other times the hands worked at night in order to catch up on work which they were failing to complete during the regular working hours. On March 31, 1854, on the other hand, he recorded that a slave had been given a pair of shoes "For attention to Stock on Sunday." In the same month another man was paid $2.83 for "night work in shop," while five others received hats for their night work. In the next month, a Negro worked sixteen nights and was paid the sum of $6.00 for having worked on his own time. This wage amounted to 37½c per night.

Under ordinary circumstances the Negroes could confidently expect payment for extra work, but whenever they got behind on their tasks, or the weather did not permit them to work out-of-doors throughout the day, they could also expect to work at night without pay. In emergencies they often toiled after dark and this was especially true during the winter months. Night jobs were done regularly then as a matter of course, for it was at this period of the year when many of the necessary repairs to equipment and buildings were made. Winter jobs performed at night included repair of plow stocks, work on the chimneys and floors of the slave cabins, making hoes, hoe handles and axe helves, storing away planks and lumber, and shucking corn and platting shucks for use in making baskets and horse collars.

Once when Davis was having overseer trouble his Negroes had to work nearly every night throughout an entire month in order to catch up on jobs which were supposed to have been completed during the day time. No extra pay was received by the Negroes in this case.

Throughout his ownership of Beaver Bend, Davis allowed some of his Negroes to purchase articles on credit from the plantation. The article most often purchased was chewing tobacco, and the slaves were required to pay for it when they were paid for extra work or whenever they were rewarded for having done a job well. This latter practice of paying the Negroes for doing good work was followed consistently by Davis. On April 14, 1856, for example, he wrote, "I promised my men if my [cotton] crop is kept clean of grass & weeds—to allow them to Sell a waggon load of watermelons for *their* benefit, the money to be divided among the *men*." This promise was carried out, for a few months afterwards when watermelons came in the Negroes were allowed to take one hundred watermelons to Marion, where they sold the watermelons and divided the proceeds. At another time Davis gave a dollar to a young Negro for mending an old barouche. As late as 1861, Old Sol was rewarded for having caught eight polecats which had been killing chickens.

Another manner in which the slaves came into possession of small sums of money resulted from their owner's habit of allowing them to share in certain of the plantation crops. The first instance of this policy was in 1850, when eight Negro men were permitted to share in the cotton crop. Their portion amounted to 3,404 pounds of cotton, approximately seven bales if this were lint cotton, and they were paid two cents per pound for it, or a total of $68.08. The practice of sharing crops with the Negroes was again referred to when Davis drew up his list of rules for his slaves' conduct in 1851. Later, in 1857, he began turning over to the Negroes a piece of land which they worked for their own benefit. As he described the plan, on April 24, all profit from the slaves' land was to be divided "according to the work—their behaviour,—their married or Single condition—In Such way that good work and good Conduct Shall receive Suitable preferences—The land to be worked by all in Common & in my time— No work of nights or Sundays—nor when my cotton is grassy in the drill." As it happened, while this plan was in effect Davis' cotton did become grassy and as a result the Negroes were unable to work their cotton on their master's time. He compromised with them nevertheless, by giving them half holidays from their regular work which they employed in working their crop. Moreover, the experiment did not prove profitable for the slaves, for their land produced only 1,772 pounds of seed cotton, or approximately one bale weighing five hundred pounds. Davis was disappointed with the unfortunate outcome, writing in his farm book on December 19, that the output "was much less than I expected the ground to produce when it was first planted." After 1857 the Negroes were allowed to share every year in the peanut and pea crops rather than the cotton, and were permitted to transport their peanuts and peas to Marion where they sold the produce for their own benefit.

On occasions Davis followed still another common practice of rewarding his slaves, namely: either to divide them into gangs and allow the gangs to compete for a prize, or to conduct a contest in which a prize was offered to the individual winner. Both practices were commonly pursued during the cotton picking months, for of more importance to Davis than rewarding his slaves was the fact that as a result of their contests they accomplished more work, which of course was advantageous to him. The custom was mentioned as early as the cotton picking season of 1851, when nine slaves were placed in each of two gangs. Two Negroes, Wash and Joe, served as leaders of their respective groups. Two and a half pounds of tobacco was promised to the gang picking the largest amount of cotton during the week of the contest. From Davis' standpoint the contest was exceedingly profitable. The contestants picked out 12,762 pounds of cotton, the largest ever gathered in one week at the plantation to that date. One side picked 6,470 pounds, the other picked 6,292 pounds, thus indicating the keen rivalry which existed among the participants of the contest. Later, in the last week of September, 1859, one of the many later contests was held, at which time the winning team picked the following exceptional amounts:

	Monday	Tuesday	Wednesday	Thursday	Friday	Saturday	
Lucy	350	402	407	405	370	457	2,391
Wash	299	339	297	369	322	368	1,994
Joe	263	305	372	321	334	381	1,976
Riner	360	309	351	321	316	278	1,935
Johnson	256	300	346	320	290	376	1,888
Hanover	268	259	361	268	307	360	1,823

This kind of competition, once inaugurated, was nurtured at Beaver Bend and Davis, like most of the planters of the blackbelt, used it to his own advantage. He had some good pickers and boasted about them whenever the opportunity arose. Perhaps he made wagers with his neighbors that his slaves could outpick theirs and took part in inter-plantation cotton picking contests, for such betting was not uncommon. Certainly he could have won many bets with such an incomparable picker as Lucy.

Another type of contest, one between individual slaves, was first announced at Beaver Bend on Monday, September 8, 1856, when Davis promised to "give the choice hat to that hand which picks the greatest excess this week over his or her Monday's work provided that Monday's work was over or to 200 [pounds of cotton] & provided we get 24,000 [pounds] this week." On the day the contest was announced eight Negroes had picked two hundred or more pounds of cotton, and therefore they were in competition for the hat. During the week of the contest, according to Davis, the eight contestants and sixteen other hands "picked out 25,245 lbs.—far the best week's work ever done on this place—All hands were well—every day clear and hot." This was good cotton picking. That the contest was profitable for Davis in the amount of cotton picked is shown by the fact that in the preceding week the Negroes had picked only 9,880 pounds during four and a half day's work; and that in the full week following the contest they picked out only 17,789 pounds. All this for a hat, although Lucy, who won it with ease, could feel proud of it because it became a badge of honor.

At the end of the contest Davis indulged in another of his methods of keeping his Negroes satisfied. On Saturday noon, when the competition ended, he announced a half holiday and added that he "was very anxious to have them dance at night—unusually anxious." According to him, "The dance continued till late." Incidently, this custom of giving half holidays as well as holidays was practiced consistently by Davis. The holidays usually came at the ends of weeks when the slaves had done good work, such as in the above instance, on important days of the year, after the crops had been laid by, sometimes during wet weather when the Negroes could not get out-of-doors to work, and always at Christmas. Especially during the Christmas season the more trustworthy Beaver Bend slaves were allowed to go "marketing" in Marion or Hamburg. If work at the plantation was so pressing at Christmas time that it had to be finished, the slaves had to stay at home and work. But on those few occasions during the holiday season when they remained at their tasks they were paid for their labor. In 1856, for example, eleven slaves worked at fifty cents to a dollar a day, and for their work were paid a total of $31.76 in cash.

All of these features of control over the slaves led to Davis' own profit. Of equal importance was his system of appointing each slave to perform a certain job or jobs. It is of course true that in this he was not alone, for specialization among plantation Negroes was commonly practiced by Southern planters. If some such system had not been devised, the slaves could never have developed into efficient or even acceptable workers. In keeping with this plan, most of the Beaver Bend slaves were grouped into two divisions: the regulars and irregulars. In addition, there were the house servants who performed the usual household duties of maids, cooks, butlers, houseboys, and other domestics. Generally speaking, the regulars hoed and plowed, and those blacks who were not intelligent enough to perform these important tasks in an acceptable manner were placed in the trash gang. The jobs of this last group were to pick up trash, sweep the yards, help clear land, and to perform other such lowly tasks. The hoe and plow hands were probably the most important at Beaver Bend, for it was essential that their work be performed correctly if the plantation was to be successful and show a profit. They and their work always received major attention and supervision from Davis and the overseers.

The irregular hands were the skilled laborers, performing the most exacting jobs on the place aside from hoeing and plowing. Their tasks, as well as the jobs of certain other slaves are indicated by the following significant chart which has been taken directly from the Davis farm book, under the date of January 3, 1861. The information contained in the chart is especially worthwhile because it was written down late in the ante-bellum period. It thus shows precisely the high degree of specialization which Davis had developed among his Negroes at Beaver Bend after thirteen years experience as a planter. For this reason, if for no other, the chart is quite valuable. Included in it are the particular jobs assigned to each of the more important plantation hands, as well as Davis' opinion of some of his Negroes. No mention is made of the house servants, the members of the trash gang, the children, or of any of the slaves who at the time were living at the Davis town house in Marion:

List of hands on plantation:

Regulars	Wash,ton	leader	[0] + Lucy	
	+ Joe		0 Amy	
	8 Dick	hog feeder	+ Hester	
	8 Harrison		Peggy	
	+ Johnson	leader	Amelio	
	+ Ewel		+ Rino	
	00 Pompey		+ Hanah	
	00 Poldo	ditcher	+ Lizzy	
	00 Alix	wagoner	0 Sophronia	
	+ Hanover		0 Liyett	
	08 Thom		Eliza Ann	½ suckler
	+ Ambrose	wagoner	+ Henrieta	
	+ Sam		+ Adaline	½
	+ George	Giner	Margret	½
	08 May		Letty	½
	08 William		8 Kelly	½
			08+ Old Sol	½
			08 Milly	½

Irregulars	Y Sol	carriage driver orchardist blacksmith currier	
	Spot	ox driver orchardist Stableman till Sunrise	
	Wright	house carpenter	
	Eliza Wright	cook & food carrier	
	Julia	water & food carrier	
	Hyram	sheep driver fire maker etc.	) helps
	Betty	water & food carrier	} at the
	Y Milly	milker	) hoe

8 These are regular hoe hands
0 These have tar on their fingers [meaning they stole or were good cotton pickers]
+ These are regular plough hands

Although quite valuable, the above chart by no means indicates all of the jobs performed by the Negroes. Aside from their regular plantation duties they were often loaned by Davis for work on community projects such as the construction of school and church buildings. Another task which they performed every year was work on the public roads in the neighborhood of Beaver Bend. According to law, each planter was expected to furnish annually a portion of his Negroes for this work. In fact, every adult male was expected to put in a few days each year on the roads. The matter was directed locally by the county governments throughout the state. The service of all physically fit males was required, although in Perry County persons over the age of forty-five were exempted. Boards of apportioners were appointed by the County Commissioners for the purpose of deciding on the number of days and the number of slaves each planter was to furnish for the job. Davis' first reference to his Negroes' working on the public roads was made in January, 1853. In December of the same year a few of his hands worked on the roads for a period of ten days. In March, 1854, nine hands worked and a wagon was furnished, too. During August, 1855, eight men, four mules, and two plows were supplied from Beaver Bend. Nine hands performed the task from December 3 through December 7, of the same year. Seven worked during April, 1857; and in April, 1859, eighteen were at work at one time. These, however, are random examples. The Davis slaves put in road duty every year.

Moreover, during the course of a typical year the slaves at Beaver Bend performed dozens of jobs. The year was usually started off with the clearing of new land to be cultivated in cotton. January was one of the busiest months of the year. After the trees on new land were felled, shingles were cut, rails split, fences constructed and repaired, and firewood cut. Fruit trees and hedge were planted and sometimes replanted; work was done on the public road; cabin yards raked and cleaned off; logs, trash, and brush piled and burned; ditches dug; old cotton seed and corn stalks either plowed under or pulled up and burned; cotton ginned and hauled away to be sold; grain crops sowed; peas beat out; hogs killed and the meat salted away; corn shelled; collars, ropes, harness, shovels, and bricks made; cabins constructed and repaired; gates and bridges built and repaired; gullies and washes filled; spinning and weaving done; clothes cut out; skins dressed; and great quantities of animal manure hauled to the various sections of the plantation. The slaves had a busy time in the first month of the year. Toward the end of the month the plows were started, and in February the work of the first month was continued whenever necessary. A typical February's work was described, March 1, 1861, by an overseer, "This has been a pleasant month for work— I have bedded up about 175 acres of corn. . . . I have got all my old corn land Reddy for planting. On the 25 and 26 of this mont I planted 7 acres of corn—Stopt until the 2 of March—Maid 460 log heapes burnt all the loges and all the trash. . . . Hauled 83 loades of maneur—26 loades of Railes—24 loades of wood—bilt Twenty one Hundred yds of fence part of which was washt away by the Rise of the River—Split Some few Rails—Cut old loges in diferent places—Knocked [down] about half my cotton Stalks. Sowed 23 bushels of oates—made a finish of the Saw mill. We ar know reddy to go to bedding up our new grounds—we have not bed up any cotton land yet. Hour Stock of all kinds has improved Sum for the last month. Had very little Sickness among our niggers during the month."

Additional land was usually bedded for cotton during the month of March, and the corn planting was completed. Potatoes were set. More manure was hauled to the fields. Some ditches were deepened as the necessity arose, and gates and fences were built or repaired. Cabbage plants were set out and the garden plots planted during the month and continued into April. Plowing, however, was the chief work ordinarily done in March and April. During April and May the cotton was planted. So were watermelons. The important job, as cotton came up, was to keep the crop free from grass. Because of the location of Beaver Bend, grass was often extremely troublesome and the task of killing it was always given great attention. The jobs of plowing and hoeing thus were often continued well into July. On those occasions when late frosts came it was necessary to replant both corn and cotton. In July and August, fodder was pulled, stacked, and stored away for use during the winter. By September some of the cotton was usually ready to be picked. Picking continued until about the middle of December, or until the job was completed, and in a few instances it was necessary to pick until about the middle of January. In November and December the slave women cut out and sewed together winter clothes for the slaves. Some weaving was done. The men started their winter "job work," which kept them occupied until or into January of the new year. On December 10, 1853, an ordinary day of the last month of the year was described by an overseer: "Run the gin—burned brush—Split rails—Salted meat—run wagon, hauled wood—made pig pen . . . boiled corn for hogs—daubed house."

Davis was usually proud of his Negroes for the excellent manner in which they performed their jobs, and he often made complimentary remarks in his farm book about the superior quality of the work done by them. An example is a statement made on July 9, 1852, on his return to Beaver Bend after a short absence: "more had been done than I expected—well done thou good and faithful servants." Nevertheless, it was to be expected that at times his Negroes would demon-

strate a lazy attitude toward their tasks, and on occasions they did indeed become careless in their work. Frequently their carelessness resulted in a monetary loss to the plantation. At times they also worked
slowly at their jobs, but this, too, was to be expected. Ordinarily,
however, they were good workers, and on the whole the available records show that they were as efficient as could be expected. They
were treated in a fair manner and usually with great leniency by their
master. The fact that Davis established rather easy rules for their
conduct, housed them well, clothed and fed them acceptably, paid
them for extra work, and in general was a kind master, must have all
had a share in inducing them to work to the best of their ability.
There is no reason to doubt that their master was a good one. They
on their part demonstrated their appreciation by executing his orders
as best they knew how.

———— 6

PURCHASE OF SUPPLIES AND SUBSISTENCE FARMING

I Hope before many years that we neighbors will be able to show off not only our Cotton & Corn, but our hog pens—our blooded cows, Sheep etc., Setting a good example & increasing our Comforts. We Shall See." In these words, written on July 19, 1856, after completing one of the many tours of his plantation, Davis expressed one of his fondest desires. He wanted self-sufficiency above all things at Beaver Bend and attempted to the best of his ability to attain it. But there was something wrong—he could never attain his ideal and in no year was he able to operate Beaver Bend without spending large sums of money for various plantation supplies. His hopes were never fulfilled because he followed the custom of his contemporaries—he always concentrated on the production of cotton—it was his practice each year to put slightly more than half of his tillable land in the white staple. Unlike some of his fellow planters, however, he did strive conscientiously year by year to diversify his farming activities more and more, but like them he needed cash money if he hoped to continue operating his place. The strong profit motive in raising cotton was also too much for him to resist. Seeking monetary profits he lost self-sufficiency. Such was the case with nearly all cotton planters of his period.

Most cotton plantations of the ante-bellum South were not self-sufficient; and this is true in spite of the wide-spread and popular belief, augmented by stories of ill-informed creative writers and others, that nearly every article needed on a plantation was produced there. The traditional Deep South planter has been unfortunately described as a goateed nabob, living in a magnificient, columned mansion approached by a private road, and having all of this earth's blessings showered on him for the asking. Slaves and "mammies" and faithful butlers and valets are supposed to have worked diligently and only for his comforts. He had all of life's luxuries, fine horses, beautiful women, wines and liquors, and great wealth. Such a description may be quite correct in isolated cases, but more often a planter was only a very serious minded agriculturist, interested primarily in the weather, his friends, his crops, and how to stay out of debt. He was no different from most other people. He had his calling—usually raising cotton, sugar, or rice. If he wished to satisfy a desire for certain luxuries he had to buy them. He could no more produce even his necessities than can the average planter today. His annual procedure was to plunge heavily into the production of his staple, to hope for good prices, to go to church, to curse the weather, to use his credit to provision his establishment until crops were ready for sale, and to rely almost entirely upon proceeds from sales of produce to get out of debt at the end of the season.

Hugh Davis was no different from other planters, unless it be that he did finally manage to get out of debt and that he was smart enough to work consciously toward producing numerous plantation necessities which many other planters purchased. As the decade of the fifties progressed he bought fewer and fewer supplies, and produced some articles so successfully that it was not necessary to supplement them through purchases. Nevertheless, included in his personal papers and correspondence are receipted bills for more than ten thousand dollars paid out for supplies between 1848 and 1862. Even this figure can not include all that was expended on supplies, and it seems quite certain that he annually averaged more than one thousand dollars in expenditures for his supplies.

When Davis took over Beaver Bend he necessarily had to obtain rather large supplies with which to inaugurate operations. He had little available cash money for the purpose, but fortunately for him the South had developed an elaborate credit system and economy which afforded him the opportunity to take up planting. Even his land could not rightly be called his own, for the several notes given in payment of parts of his property were not paid off until 1852. He was in debt for slaves obtained in 1847 and 1848. Moreover, he owed several large accounts at Marion mercantile establishments. But regardless of his heavy debts he went ahead with his new venture with the expectation of paying himself out of debt with proceeds from cotton to be made during the first years at his plantation. Worse luck for him, cotton brought low prices in 1848, and at the end of the year his debts had increased still more. Perhaps more depressing were reports which came about hard times in Mobile. Even in 1847, he had been informed that commercial failures and extreme money pressure in England were causing "a gloom and depression rarely witnessed" in the Alabama cotton town, and that as a result money was extremely tight. The mid-century revolutions in Europe also helped to contract cotton markets in the United States, and Alabama and Mobile suffered along with other cotton producing areas and markets.[1]

There is little wonder that Davis stuck to his law practice for a few years after he began his planting activities, for without the income derived from his practice he could not have continued at Beaver Bend unless he had been willing to plunge still farther into debt. On the other hand there were several factors working in his favor, and of particular significance was the very fact that he could obtain credit with ease. He owned rather extensive town properties in Marion, among them being several buildings which were rented to business firms. A number of undeveloped town lots were also owned. Some property was owned in Centerville, a town near Marion. He also had a small forge in operation in the nearby town of Montevallo. The forge was sold in 1848 to tide him over, however. Ownership of these various properties and prospects of some profits from his plantation gave him a good credit rating. His personal reputation as a lawyer and the good name of his wife's family were also important in inducing merchants to advance credit. Of special significance, too, was the custom of expecting men of his class of society to pay their honest debts.[2]

[1]For an excellent account of European influences on American cotton markets, see Thomas P. Martin, "Cotton and Wheat in Anglo-American Trade and Politics, 1846-1852," *Journal of Southern History*, I (August, 1935), 293-319, and his "Conflicting Cotton Interests at Home and Abroad, 1848-1857," *ibid.*, VII (May, 1941), 173-194.

[2]For an account of the code of a Southern gentleman in the ante-bellum period,

Since 1842, Davis had bought rather large quantities of household necessities from Fry and Craig (later Fry, Bliss and Company), one of the leading commission merchant houses in Mobile. His relations with the firm had always been good, and for several years during the 1840's he had been retained by the company to collect its accounts with negligent customers in Perry County. As a result of this former connection with the establishment, it was willing to extend him credit after he turned to planting. Another important Mobile organization with which he had had business relations was Stringfellow and Hanna, both members of the firm being from Davis' own county. This Company and others sought his business in 1848 and afterwards, and at various times he received invitations from merchants in New Orleans, Selma, and Montgomery to use his credit with them. It is sufficient to say that from the beginning Davis had no trouble whatsoever in obtaining whatever credit he needed from his commission merchants. Besides, he could always depend on the merchants of Marion, with whom he had had extensive relations since his arrival in the town in 1834. From them he had purchased such articles as dry goods, groceries and household furniture, and many of them (at times under different names) had allowed him to buy on time. They had frequently advanced him small sums of money. They continued to do both after 1848, and from them he obtained a large portion of his plantation supplies.

Davis' affairs with the Marion merchants are of interest because they furnish an excellent example of the extent to which a planter could sometimes operate on credit. Among the local business firms with which he traded were Napoleon Lockett, Wyatt and Houston, Blount and Tutt, Brown and Fowlkes,[3] Eli Loveland and Company,[4] King, Upson and Company,[5] and W. B. and T. Lawson. An illustra-

see Charles S. Syndor, "The Southerner and the Laws," *Journal of Southern History,* VI (February, 1940), 3-23.

[3]Samuel H. Fowlkes, of Brown and Fowlkes, was an outstanding Marion merchant. Much of his merchandise was bought in New York City, and he travelled there each winter at least from 1847 through 1856. He was back again in 1866. Samuel H. Fowlkes to Mary A. Fowlkes, Feb. 23, 1847; Feb. 22, 1854; Feb. 26, 1856; Feb. 22, 1866, in Fowlkes Papers.

[4]In 1839, Davis bought $237.50 worth of furniture from Eli Loveland and $241.64 from Wyatt and Houston. A typical business transaction was completed with Loveland in 1839: "By the 1st January next I promise to pay William Simonton or bearer the Sum of Sixty Seven dollars for note of Giles N. Langdon this day Credited on my account with Eli Loveland & Co. This 17th day of July 1839. Hugh Davis." Davis Papers.

[5]On April 29, 1840, King, Upson and Company sold its accounts, amounting to

tion of the way Davis used his credit to stay in the planting business is his relations with Wyatt and Houston. In 1848, he owed the firm for goods purchased since 1844, but despite his inability to pay the company anything on his account it advanced him credit for $147.31 worth of dry goods in his first year as a planter. On January 1, 1849, he made arrangements to pay off the account by turning over two notes amounting to $215.97, due him for legal services, and gave his own note of $607.26, due January 1, 1850, for the balance. From January 1, 1849 through April 28, 1853, the company again carried him without his making a single payment on account. On the latter date his four-year old account was paid with a note of $636.79. Another example of the amount of credit that a planter could obtain is demonstrated by Davis' business with Blunt and Tutt. Between January, 1850 and January, 1855, he bought plantation supplies costing $3,404.99, including interest, from the company, and during the entire five-year period not one cash payment on account was made! In 1853, however, part of the bill was settled when Davis sold a town lot in Marion, for one thousand dollars, to one of the members of the firm. Then, on January 1, 1855, rents from two store buildings were turned over to the company, but the sum of $1,086.47 was still owed. Afterwards, Davis paid a little better, for on January 25, 1856, he recorded in his farm book that he "Went to Marion—carried the wagon & bought Supplies of merchandise for the Season—Such as Towells— Calicoes—Tobacco—nails, mud boots—etc. etc., about $80. . . . Drew on Mr Pleasant [his Mobile cotton factor] for $800 in favor of Blount."

For a year before assuming actual possession of Beaver Bend, Davis bought up supplies to be used after starting operations. In January, 1847, he purchased seventeen hogs to fatten for killing in order that he might have some meat supply during his first year at the plantation. Large amounts of nails, lumber, and other building materials were obtained. Then, in January, 1848, he bought six mules for $562.50; a wagon, $130.00; corn, fodder and plantation implements, $550.78; a yoke of oxen, $40.00; and 4,500 pounds of pork, $191.70. Shortly afterwards, he paid $140.00 for two more mules. From Fry, Bliss and Company he obtained during the rest of the year such articles

$53,539.16, to a Marion merchant named Napoleon Lockett. Perry County, Deed Record, E, 364-371.

as potatoes, buckwheat, molasses, vinegar, flour, candles, sugar, salt, brown sugar, bacon sides, rice, and oysters. Locally, he bought fodder, corn, foodstuffs, dry goods, medicines, and other supplies.

The year 1848 was indeed an expensive one for the fledgling planter. Lists of many of his annual purchases are available and could be enumerated in detail year by year, but such a procedure is omitted because it seems both unnecessary and monotonous. Let it suffice to reiterate that Davis bought large quantities of plantation supplies each year and that on the basis of available, although incomplete, records he annually expended considerably more than one thousand dollars on the purchases. It is possible, however, that expenses were not quite so high in 1859 and 1860, for the Davis papers and farm books of those years contain relatively few entries about purchases of supplies. It may be that most of the needed supplies were made at home and that at last Beaver Bend became almost self-sufficient. On the other hand, it is also possible that as a result of Davis' absence during part of the two-year period, proper entries were not made in the farm books. Davis himself had become an invalid and could not give undivided attention to his affairs. Under ordinary circumstances at Beaver Bend, he and his overseers maintained an extraordinarily complete written record of events, but in Davis' absence and incapacitation from June, 1859 to June, 1860, his overseers neglected to write in as much detail in the farm books as formerly. For these reasons, even if it is certain that fewer supplies were bought in 1859 and 1860 than at any other period, it seems unwise to conclude that Beaver Bend ever approached self-sufficiency during Davis' ownership.

Most supplies bought in Mobile after 1843 came from Fry, Bliss and Company and from Gates and Pleasant Company. A few purchases were made in the seaport town from Loughry and Homer. In addition to the Marion merchants already mentioned, some supplies were obtained from William Saunders, John H. Elliot, I. Catlin, and J. G. Brazelton. W. J. Norris and Company, of Selma, also sold Davis some articles. From all of these concerns he bought such items as the following: corn, pork, salt, fodder, whiskey, molasses, cloth, shoes, hats, medicines, bagging, rope, twine, dishes, furniture, bricks, livestock, iron, lumber, dry goods, cauldrons, nails, farm implements, sugar, cheese, buckwheat, potatoes, flour, candles, rice, peas, kitchen utensils, crockery, coffee, tobacco, pickles, bridles and other leather

goods, syrup, butter, vinegar, lime, nutmeg, pocket knives, boot black-
ing, eggs, oysters, and sardines. At frequent intervals his Mobile factors and commission merchants forwarded him a *Price-Current,* published weekly, containing prices current of all plantation supplies
which planters ordinarily purchased. Included also was information
on weekly receipts of the articles at Mobile, as well as tables indicating
amounts received during the previous market season. Receipts, prices
and exports of cotton were also indicated, and in general the *Price-
Current* contained information of significant interest to the planter.
Davis no doubt pored over the contents avidly, looking for bargains,
trying to out-figure the market. As one authority on Southern history has stated, "It is clear that the *Price-Current* did not make enter-
taining reading, for editorials, political news, and international relations were not paraded on its pages, but the farmer and the factor
scanned them with interest, for the information they yielded spelled
profit or ruin to both."[6]

Davis' method of paying his plantation accounts is both interesting
and enlightening. It might be added, too, that the credit system of
which he and other planters were a part has recently attracted great
attention among students of the history of the ante-bellum South.
Serving as his agents were cotton factors with headquarters in Mobile.
These hardy individuals were among the most active business men in
the South. Their chief function was to sell cotton for planters of the
interior, but they were often bankers, banking representatives, merchants, salesmen, agricultural advisers, and close friends of the planters
they represented. A large portion of them being members of planter
families, they frequently also were blood relations of many of their
clients. As business men they were of first-rate importance. Because
of the credit system that they helped evolve in co-operation with their
planter friends, they were as much responsible as any one group for
the growth and maintainence of the whole cotton economy and plantation system as developed in Alabama and other Southern states in the
ante-bellum period.

Moreover, factors were just as important to rice and sugar plantations as they were to cotton plantations. In the colonial period of
American history they had been active in the tobacco business in the

[6]Wendell H. Stephenson, "Ante-Bellum New Orleans as an Agricultural Focus,"
Agricultural History, XV (October, 1941), 172-173.

Upper South, and with the coming of extensive cotton production
some of them had turned to the selling of the white staple. When
planters moved in large numbers to Alabama during and after the
War of 1812, factors moved with them, and by the time Davis became
a planter the factorage system was well organized in his state. The
intrepid business men were city builders and it is they, more than any
others, who raised Mobile to its position of almost incomparable
significance in the cotton business of the South before 1860. By the
time Hugh Davis opened Beaver Bend there were dozens of factors in
Mobile. Only New Orleans could boast of greater business transactions in cotton. That great city drew its business from the Mississippi Valley, however, while Mobile depended for the most part on
Alabama, whose Alabama and Tombigbee river systems naturally fun-
neled heavy traffic to the port.

Davis' method of paying an account with a factor was quite simple.
He wrote either to his factor or commission merchant (often a factor
was also a commission merchant), and put in an order for certain
supplies. If the goods were obtained through a commission merchant,
one of two methods of payment was usually employed. Either the
merchant informed Davis of the cost of the articles and requested
that a draft be forwarded to pay the cost, plus a commission of 2½%,
or presented a bill to Davis' factor. If the latter were the case, the
factor paid the bill and debited Davis' account with the amount of the
cost, which was in effect an extension of credit until some of the
Beaver Bend cotton was sold. If a draft were forwarded to a merchant it was presented to the factor for payment and after accepting
the draft the factor debited it against Davis. Money thus advanced
of course drew interest until settlement was made, and therefore the
planter paid the usual premium for the use of articles obtained on
credit. Moreover, as was to be expected, credit prices were somewhat
higher than cash prices. The whole system was not at all economical
for the planter, but he employed it because he was an intregal part of
an agricultural society living almost entirely on credit. During certain seasons of a year even a highly successful planter often went for
weeks without a single piece of cash money on hand. Loans of twenty-
five cents and fifty cents made by men owning thousands of acres of
land and dozens of slaves were not at all uncommon during the ante-
bellum period. Davis himself made many such loans. Be that as it

may, whenever he needed plantation supplies his wants were under-
written on time by his factors.

What else could the factor do?   As mentioned above, his very
existence as a business figure depended on such advances.   Both the
factor and the commission merchant stood to lose heavily on some of
the drafts which they accepted, for there were of course always the
possibilities of fraud, default, bankruptcy, dishonesty, and, worst of
all, crop failure or sale of cotton at low prices.   Moreover, many
planters were notoriously extravagant and often plunged deeply into
debt in their purchases of slaves, land, farm implements, and plantation supplies.   On the other hand, the personal honesty and general
God-fearing characteristics of the planter were in favor of the factor.
A factor's complete willingness to trust his clientele is well illustrated
by a short note written to Davis in February, 1856.   Davis had just
involved himself in one of the luxuries of planters—he had bought
some slaves on credit and had paid for them with drafts.   The factor
wrote, "Your favor of 2nd Inst. came to hand yesterday [February
10] to which we reply that you need give yourself no uneasiness as to
the drafts—both have been paid, and as yet we have not Suffered by
it. Should we be unable to get on Without it we will let you know. . . ."

Goods purchased in Mobile were shipped by river boat from that
place to Cahaba or Selma, and were usually insured by Davis against
loss by fire or otherwise.   For nine years he insured every bill of goods
shipped to him from Mobile and, strangely enough, the only time he
failed to insure an order he presumably lost the entire bill of goods.
In April, 1856, he bought about seven hundred dollars worth of
merchandise to be shipped to Selma by river boat.   On the way up
the river the boat sank and the goods were lost.   On April 25, Davis
indignantly wrote in his farm book that "The carelessness of those in
charge of the boat caused the loss & are responsible," but as far as is
known he was never compensated for his loss.   For five years Davis
had his Mobile goods, after arrival in Selma, hauled to Beaver Bend
by freight companies operating out of the Dallas County town.   On
February 15, 1853, he finally awoke to the fact that drayage bills on
goods transported from Selma to his plantation were greatly increasing the cost of his supplies.   He had purchased fifty-one dollars worth
of goods in Mobile, to be hauled by professional freighters from Selma
to his place.   Drayage on the last leg of the trip, less than twenty

miles, cost nine dollars. Davis noted in his farm book both the cost of the merchandise and the drayage, complaining that "this last money was inconsiderately expended, and ought to have been saved—to pay nearly 1/5 the value of any article to get it hauled from Selma, Shows great want of attention to one's interest." Afterwards, at least for the next two years, whenever goods bought in Mobile were transported from Selma to Beaver Bend they were hauled in plantation wagons driven by plantation Negroes. In 1855, the Cahaba and Marion Railroad was in operation near Beaver Bend and most goods were from then on shipped from Mobile to Selma by river boat and by rail from Selma to Marion Junction to Hamburg, and from the latter place were hauled in wagons to the plantation. For example, an overseer recorded on February 15, 1858, that "4 mules & wagons [had] gone to Depot all day—brought home Iron, bridles, Shoes, bale of Oznaburg, Potatoes, & Molasses." By hauling supplies in his own wagons, Davis was able to cut down greatly on expenses, and it is rather surprising that he waited five years before taking up the practice. This determination to lower his costs of transportation may have been another reason for obtaining a large portion of his supplies from Marion merchants. Goods bought there were always hauled in wagons to Beaver Bend.

As might be expected, one of Davis' chief problems was maintenance of an adequate supply of foodstuffs for the large crowd of people connected with his establishment. Feeding approximately eighty mouths, during his last years at the plantation, was obviously one of his major considerations. Large quantities of feed also had to be provided for his livestock. Between 1848 and 1862, he expended more money for foods than for any other necessity, but this expense would have been even more exorbitant and would have reduced his profits more noticeably if he had not attempted always to produce large portions of his food stores. Meat was a particularly important item in the diet of everyone at the plantation. Large quantities of bacon and pork especially were consumed the year round, so much so that he was never able to produce all that was required. Even so, he sought consistently to raise large numbers of hogs, and always placed several of his most trusted Negroes in charge of those important animals. It will be remembered, too, that the overseer was usually rewarded for close attention to the hogs and was given a cash payment for each one hundred pounds of hog meat produced under his supervision. Hog raising at Beaver Bend was considered almost as important as cotton. In December and January of each year, hogs were killed, sausage and lard made, and soap was manufactured from the entrails. Chitlins always had a definite appeal to the slaves. Hams, reserved for use by the members of the master's family, were cured over hickory logs and packed away in casks, barrels and sacks. The containers were then filled up with ashes in order to prevent skippers and bugs and then placed in the smoke-house to be used as occasion demanded. Other parts of the hog meat were salted away in barrels to be rationed later among the slaves and overseer.

During part of each year hogs were allowed to run wild and grub for themselves in the wooded lands on or near Beaver Bend. Several times each year they were rounded up and counted, and one of Davis' most enjoyable pastimes was "hog-hunting," when he and his sons and sometimes friends and neighbors went into the woods looking for the animals. Toward the latter part of each year the hogs were confined either in pens or in a so-called "hog lot" where they were fattened for killing purposes. Other planters in the vicinity also let their animals run wild, and it was thus imperative to give each hog in the region an identifying brand or mark of some sort. In 1848, Davis' brand was "A crop & slet in the right ear & A Slet & hole in the left ear." Sometime later this was "changed in the left ear to a crop and a hole." But of special interest is Davis' method of feeding his hogs. Fruits were given to them regularly, when in season, with apples being used most frequently. In this connection, it was recorded in the farm book in the first week of July, 1850, that "Apples are fed to Hogs & brought to the kitchen for the hands. They are not allowed to go into the orchard. This is a good rule & must be enforced."

Davis' scientific bent was again demonstrated by his various experiments with feeds for his plantation hogs. On November 15, 1850, he put his "hogs in the pea field to fatten—a fine quality," adding "I wish to fatten them on the pea exclusively—see if this is done." There is no record available of the outcome of this experiment, but it must not have been completely gratifying because several other feeds were later tried out. The peanut in particular was fed to the animals for a few years, but in 1858 it was concluded that the peanut was not as good as the pea. Davis wondered why this was the case, but never found the answer. Meanwhile, other experiments were being made. One preparation, concocted in 1854, consisted of four bushels of cotton seed and one bushel of potatoes boiled together in a cauldron. On November 13, 1855, it was recorded that the Negroes had "commenced boiling corn for fattening hogs. . . . The plan is to boil corn & pumpkins, but I need another cauldron—So that as one heats, the other may cool." This effort did not prove satisfactory and from 1855 to 1862 the customary food consisted of a mixture of boiled corn and cotton seed. Peas in the raw were also given to the hogs. It is quite probable also that other feeds were placed before the animals, but there are no records available to prove it.

One problem which Davis never solved at Beaver Bend was that of his hogs' habit of eating their pigs and as late as February 27, 1859, an overseer reported that he had "lost 8 pigs by hog eating." The next day he lamented, "I found 9 more pigs dead by their mothers lying on them, surely we have the worse luck with hog than any body else—sows have fine litter of pigs then turn around and eat them— why it is I cannot tell. I never knew so much of it before in all my hog raising but What cannot be remedied must be submitted to." Despite such disasters, large quantities of hog meat were made annually at Beaver Bend, and Davis developed quite a local reputation as a successful hog breeder. On several occasions animals belonging to other planters were put with his hogs to improve the stock. Some idea of meat production at his plantation may be gained by the following table. The figures should not be taken as complete, however, because some were left out of the farm books:

Date		Number of Hogs	Weight in Pounds
1850 Dec.	1	17	2,000
1853 Jan.	3	48	6,844
Dec.	9	25	1,807
1854 Dec.	29	54	5,912
Dec.	30	12	2,173
1855 Dec.	31	—	5,641
1856 Dec.	3	37	5,504
Dec.	22	—	2,253
1857 Dec.	24	2	340
Dec.	25	20	3,284
1858 Jan.	6	29	3,769
Jan.	16	13	2,355

1859	Jan.	3	40	6,757
	Jan.	15	25	3,307
	Feb.	3	6	610
	Dec.	7	20	3,018
	Dec.	21	40	4,992
1860	Jan.	2	40	4,281
	Dec.		74	9,745
				74,592

The above table shows that as the years went by, Davis produced more and more hog meat, with the 1858-1859 and 1859-1860 seasons being most successful. On February 3, 1859, it was reported that the plantation that year had made "in all 11,104 lbs. of pork, 1000 lbs. more than was ever killed before." In 1859-1860, even better luck was had, for hogs weighing 12,227 pounds were killed. Even these large totals, however, did not supply all the meat needed and, as in previous years, the stores on hand had to be supplemented by purchases. It will be noted by the table that the 1850 production was small; as a result it was necessary to purchase at least 4,500 pounds in the first part of 1851 to get through the year. Moreover, on November 17, Davis wrote his Mobile factor, "If the Bacon market is low, get me 7 or 800 lbs. of Middlings of good quality that is free from ribs—The drought of last year Shortened my allowance of Hogs and Hominy." Even in 1859, good year that it was, the meat made at home had to be supplemented by more than one thousand pounds. In 1860, over two thousand pounds were purchased. Slaves were of course more numerous during these years than at any other time and more meat was required for their consumption. Still, it seems that the overseers might have managed better.

Other meat producing animals besides hogs were raised at Beaver Bend. Large numbers of turkeys and chickens were always maintained, and sheep were to be found among the stock every year. The largest number of sheep owned at one time, in June, 1854, however, amounted only to seventy-two. Wool was used in making clothes and part of it was also usually shipped annually to Selma for sale. Some idea of the increasing interest in meat-producing livestock at the plantation may be gained by a comparison of the stock on hand in 1851 and in 1861. On January 1, 1851, there were 5 cows, 2 yearlings, 4 calves, 1 boar, 11 shoats, 21 pigs, 31 sheep, and 16 lambs. On January 1, 1861, according to a count made by the overseer, there were

"Milk cows 8—Calves 8—Heifers 4—Mails 2—Sheep 50—Goats 30 —two young kids—Hogs 20—Breeding Sows 50—Shoates 45—young pigs 3—mails—9 Fatning hogs— . . . total 127 hogs." These figures amply indicate that Davis tried to produce a large part of his meat supply, and when the great quantities necessary to feed his Negroes are remembered the importance of this phase of his management of Beaver Bend is readily apparent. He saved great sums of money annually as a result of his domestic meat production.

Moreover, pork, beef, mutton, and other meats were further supplemented by excellent catches of fishes taken from the Cahaba River. Very few seafoods were ever bought and then only at Christmas time, while Davis lived at his plantation. The river furnished more than enough, for it was quite common to catch thirty or forty fishes in one day in the baskets and nets thrown into the stream. They were big ones, too, as is shown by entries taken at random from the farm books. On June 18, 1852, an overseer recorded that he had "taken out 36 fishes from baskets;" three days later he had "taken 26 fish from baskets which were verry fine fish;" on July 19, he stated that he had "taken a fine parsel of fish from baskets this evening." The next day he "caught 1 fish—weighed 42 pounds which was fine." Indeed it was. Fishing was always good during the spring and summer seasons at Beaver Bend, and the Davis family enjoyed the sport to the fullest. As late as May 12, 1859, just before Davis was paralyzed, an overseer exclaimed that "Mr. Davis caught the Master cat fish of the season, weighing 31 lbs. the largest I ever saw."

The master of Beaver Bend realized that if he should ever attain any semblance of self-sufficiency he would have to make good yearly crops of corn and therefore always gave great attention to the cultivation of the grain. Some of the harvest was ground into meal for use by all the inhabitants of the plantation, with most of that for table use being ground at mills which were operated in the neighborhood. This was the method during Davis' first years at his place. Then, for a time a home-made, mule-drawn corn grinder was employed to make meal. But the outfit never proved satisfactory and was dubbed the *"Mule Killer"* by the overseers and the slaves. The mills of his friends were tried again. Finally, after great bother and loss from thefts by slaves while transporting corn and meal to and from the mills, a water powered mill was constructed at Beaver Bend. Actually, however, only a small portion of the corn was reserved for table use, most of it being used as feed for the stock.

Only seventy-five acres were planted in 1848, but in 1861 the acreage had increased, in keeping with the general enlargement of operations, to 230 acres. As far as can be ascertained, other annual acreages were as follows: 110 in 1851; 98 in 1853; 150 in 1854; 160 in 1855; 153 in 1856; 190 in 1857; 150 in 1858; 145 in 1859, and 240 in 1860. Unfortunately, the extant records on production of corn and fodder are both scanty and confusing. The production in 1850 is clear enough, for Davis reported that 1,050 bushels were made. But the next year he recorded only that fifty-five loads of unshucked corn had been made. This information is partially clarified by a statement made in 1852 that each wagon load of unhusked corn hauled from the fields made thirty bushels of shelled corn. About two months later it was estimated that each acre produced a little more than 150 bushels of shelled corn. Such an estimate of course does not agree with the other information on amounts produced. To confuse the matter still further, it was reported in 1860 that each wagon load contained between sixteen and eighteen bushels to the load. The only conclusion which seems likely is that at some time Davis changed from the use of a double to a single wagon. A determination of corn production must therefore remain unsolved, and it is possible only to refer to production as reported by Davis and his overseers and to employ their own varying units of measure.

In 1851, the plantation produced 1,650 bushels; 177 loads, or 3,510 bushels in 1852, and as described by Davis this was by far the biggest crop he had ever made; and 77 loads in 1853. Excessive frosts killed the corn planted in 1854, and it was necessary to replant. Late replanting caused a short crop, so much so that in 1855, for the only time in his career as a planter, Davis put more acres in corn than in cotton. No information is available on production in 1855, 1856 and 1857, except that in those years, respectively, 160, 153, and 190 acres were planted. In 1858, more than five thousand bushels of shelled corn were made, the total loads numbering 128. One hundred and twenty-nine loads were gathered in 1859. The 1860 crop seems to have been excellent and by July 31, fodder amounting to about 60,000 pounds had been gathered. The amount of shelled corn made is unknown, however.

Aside from corn, Davis cultivated several other grain crops, especially wheat, oats, rye, barley, and millet. His largest acreages were in 1854, when he put seventy-four acres in small grain, and in 1855, when seventy-seven acres were planted. Figures for other years are unavailable, but it is assumed that the usual acreages, after 1854, must have been about seventy acres. Sometimes the output was good, sometimes bad, but never sufficient, and every year had to be supplemented by purchases from local merchants in Marion, Hamburg and Selma, and from commission merchants and factors in Mobile. Because of rust caused by early spring rains, oats in particular always seemed to be short. On the other hand, it seems that rye and barley usually turned out much better, for small quantities of the two articles were often sold to neighbors and to local merchants in Marion and Hamburg. By 1860, acreages of oats and rye under cultivation amounted, respectively, to fifteen and four. Better luck was had with wheat than any other grain crop. In 1852, wheat was "a fine turn out;" it was "passing" in 1855; and in 1857, when 75½ bushels were made, it was "better than of former years." The year 1859 was a bad one, for when the overseer "thrashed out" the wheat he made only fifteen bushels on four acres. In this year, as in all others, wheat was hauled to a flour mill in Selma and there bartered for flour, one bushel of wheat being exchanged for thirty-five pounds of flour.

Vegetables and fruits formed other important items in the diet of the people at Beaver Bend, and production of these articles again saved big sums of money in the costs of operations. Few were ever purchased. Large amounts of peas were always planted for consumption by both the inhabitants and animals at the plantation. It was not at all unusual to plant more than one hundred acres in peas, ordinarily in conjunction with corn. Pumpkins and watermelons were raised every year. Among the vegetables grown every year were: cucumbers, tomatoes, egg plant, squash, okra, snap beans, butter beans, cabbage, collards, turnips, mustard, potatoes, muskmelons, and red pepper.

Exact acreages of vegetables each year are unknown, although Davis did state in his "System of farming" in 1862 that enough vegetables should be planted every year "in sufficient quantities to supply the hands three times each day." Besides the plantation garden, each Negro and the overseer had a "patch." It is doubtful, however, that enough vegetables were ever raised to realize Davis' wish, but during the spring, summer and fall seasons of each year there were enough to supplement the usual diet of meat and meal. The moderate climate in the blackbelt permitted the growth of several kinds of green vegetables throughout most of the year. The slaves could never have been truly happy without their greens and in one year, 1861, they set out 3,311 collard and 2,050 cabbage plants. Potatoes afforded another delight for the people at Beaver Bend. In fact, Davis became quite well-known locally as a potato grower and always had plenty and every year sold some to merchants in nearby towns and to planters near his place. During approximately half of his residence at Beaver Bend he also produced most of the rice consumed there. Trees of various kinds furnished most of the fruits needed. One hundred peach trees were set out in 1852, and others were added in 1854, 1856, and 1860. Other types planted were walnut, crab apple, cherry, almond, Catawba grape, mock orange, and apple. In 1860, an already large vineyard was enlarged when 336 additional vines were set out. Small quantities of these fruits were sold, but most of the produce was canned and consumed at the plantation.

All of the articles which have been mentioned, in addition to others which were possibly made, were of course of first-rate importance to Davis in that they helped him to reduce the enormous expenses entailed in the operation of a place the size of Beaver Bend. Without his production of meats and other foodstuffs he would have been in an impossible situation, or perhaps in the same position as many of his contemporaries who gave too little attention to subsistence farming and were never able to make ends meet. Cotton could rarely carry the entire load. Even so, as witnessed by the account already given of his annual expenditures and despite his varied agricultural interests, he was never able to live entirely at home. It is quite probable that he could have become much more self-sufficient if he had given more attention to hogs, stock, vegetables and fruit trees, but it must be remembered that he was operating a plantation to make money. In order to accomplish this purpose he believed it necessary to concentrate on the production of cotton. His establishment had to pay its upkeep and some profits. He was deeply in debt during his first years as a planter and considered cotton as the only product that could relieve him of the debts he had incurred to obtain possession of his lands and slaves. He failed to produce all the supplies needed, but did so because he believed it best to give most of his attention and energy to a money crop, cotton, which he hoped would furnish profits to be employed in the purchase of certain articles which he could not make at home and of others thought to be cheaper if obtained through commission merchants. His success as a producer of cotton forms the basis of discussion in the next chapter, the last one concerning his activities. Included also will be an account of the means by which his crops were sold, as well as a description of his relations with his cotton factors in Mobile.

7

PRODUCTION AND SALE OF COTTON

S ONE STUDENT of Alabama history has so well expressed the
problem, "Cotton was the key to the whole economic situation
in ante-bellum Alabama."[1] Hugh Davis and his contemporaries needed a money crop and to them cotton was the answer to
most of their problems. It was a source of credit or collateral of
loans and it brought ready cash in the Mobile market. Its royalty
was of course questioned at times, but in certain sections of the state,
particularly in the blackbelt after 1830, it was the all-important staple.

[1]Davis, *The Cotton Kingdom in Alabama*, p. 117. For discussions of the economy and
profitability of plantation slavery, see *ibid.*, pp. 169-189; Coleman, *Slavery Times in Kentucky*, pp. 65, 142-143; Flanders, *Plantation Slavery in Georgia*, pp. 213-215, 220-227;
Phillips, *American Negro Slavery*, pp. 391-392; Sydnor, *Slavery in Mississippi*, pp. 181-
202; and Lewis Cecil Gray, *History of Agriculture in the Southern United States to
1860* 2 vols. (Washington, 1933), I, 476. Gray's work is considered by many experts
to be the best in print in the field of southern agricultural history. See also Lewis Cecil
Gray, "Economic Efficiency and Competitive Advantages of Slavery under the Planta-
tion System," *Agricultural History*, IV (April, 1930), 31-47; Jordan, "The Elisha F.
King Family: Planters of the Alabama Black Belt," *ibid.*, XIX (July, 1945), 152-162;
Ulrich B. Phillips, "Plantations with Slave Labor and Free," *ibid.*, XII (January, 1938),
77-95; and Robert R. Russell, "The Economic History of Negro Slavery in the United
States," *ibid.*, XI (October, 1937), 308-321, and his "The Effects of Slavery upon
Nonslaveholders in the Antebellum South," *ibid.*, XV (April, 1941), 112-126. Among
the articles that have appeared in the *Journal of Southern History* on the specific subject
of plantation economy are the following: Robert R. Russell, "The General Effects of
Slavery upon Southern Economic Progress," IV (February, 1938), 34-54; and Thomas
P. Govan, "Was Plantation Slavery Profitable," VIII (November, 1943), 513-535.

To the ordinary planter of Davis' day there was one chief concern—
to raise as much cotton as possible and thereby, it was believed, maintain the whole economic, political, and social order which the staple
had created. Here again Davis was typical of his time and place. In
his small way, he helped maintain his county as a leading cotton producing area in Alabama and his state, for a few years, as the largest
producer in the entire country. If he had not raised cotton he would
have been quite unusual. Little remains to be said on this score, these
matters having already been discussed. Still to be mentioned, however,
are the acreages of his annual crops, yearly production, transportation
to market, and sales through his cotton factors. There is also the
question of the profitability of his chosen occupation to be considered.

As has been stated previously, about half of Beaver Bend's tillable
land, aside from grazing lands, was usually put into cotton and, as
best as can be ascertained, acreages and production of the staple in
various years were as follows:

Year	Total Acres Under Plow	Acres of Cotton Under Plow	Seed Cotton Produced	Lint Cotton Produced	Number of Bales Produced
1848	276	201	......	24,688	52
1849	....	163	98,471	25,332	51
1850	....	172	115,755	31,744	62
1851	336	173	115,624	......	63
1852	....	......	117,412	......	69
1853	306	190	146,873	39,828	80
1854	390	168	138,093	......	79
1855	391	140	135,659	......	77
1856	407	170	134,878	......	75
1857	420	230	211,572	......	......
1858	453	270	245,258	......	154
1859	546	380	284,881	98,407	196
1860	530	290	253,314	......	......
1861	600	325	151,028	......	......

This material, except for the figures on total acres under plow, has
been compiled from records of daily pickings of cotton kept by overseers and from letters received by Davis from his Mobile factors. It
is regretable that the figures are not more complete, but they do furnish
information on the most important matter—the size of cotton crops
made by Davis during each year of his career as a planter. A criterion
of some value in determining more closely the production of seed and
lint cotton and bales is a statement made by Davis on August 30,
1856, and again on November 20, 1858, that 1850 pounds of seed

cotton were usually put into one bale of ginned cotton. By using common division or multiplication, as the case may be, depending upon determined information concerning bales or seed cotton produced, as indicated in the above table, one might arrive at an approximate figure on production in those years for which information is incomplete. Moreover, Davis usually tried to gin bales weighing five hundred pounds. If this had always been the case, one could easily reach approximate figures on the production of lint cotton in some years, with the aid of the table. But at times bales were short or long. Therefore the only trustworthy information on production is that included in the above figures.

Some idea of the actual method of production may be mentioned, however. Of major importance is the moderate weather of the blackbelt, for without it cotton could never have been grown acceptably. Also of importance is the fertile, loamy, although messy, soil. At Beaver Bend the business of cultivation began with the year. Old and new lands were plowed deeply in order to take up rains. In March the ridges were split open and the cotton planted in the so-called drills. After the plants reached a height of a few inches they were chopped, or thinned, and finally one plant was left in each hill. Then came the long task of killing grass. That job was done with plows and hoes, each hoe hand being responsible for twelve acres. Small plows were used to throw dirt around the plants, and plowing continued intermittently until shortly before picking time. Lastly, the cotton was picked and baled. The long picking season and other aspects of that job are indicated by the following figures:

Cotton Picking Season	Number of Picking Days	Number of Pickers	Average Number Picking	Largest Daily Total Pickings	Largest Daily Picking by One Slave
Aug. 15-Nov. 30, 1850	79	21	15	3,120	. . . . . .
Aug. 11-Dec. 10, 1851	80	24	20	2,785	241
Aug. 30-Dec. 22, 1825	62	21	15	. . . . . .	355
Aug. 29, 1853-Feb. 6, 1854	. . . .	. . . . . .	15	3,768	383
Aug. 16, 1854-Jan. 5, 1855	96	24	19	3,777	. . . . . .
Aug. 21-Nov. 26, 1855	82	22	. . . . . .	3,440	243
Aug. 25-Dec. 8, 1856	65	27	24	4,534	469
Sept. 4-Dec. 23, 1857	73	29	27	6,040	390
Aug. 23-Dec. 22, 1858	71	30	26	8,150	523
Aug. 24-Dec. 15, 1859	75	34	29	. . . . . .	457
July 31-Dec. 24, 1860	94	38	28	3,513	304

Cotton made at Beaver Bend was ginned on the premises. By December, 1850, Davis had a first-rate gin in operation and was not only ginning his own cotton but also that of several of his neighbors. Payment for this work for outsiders usually amounted to one-fourteenth of the amount ginned. Davis had a good thing in operating his gin for other planters and as a result was able to increase somewhat his annual net profits. Not only did he receive one-fourteenth of all cotton ginned for other planters and farmers who patronized his ginhouse, but he also was allowed to keep all cotton seed taken from the lint. This seed was later used as fertilizer on his crops and as food for his hogs. Moreover, Negroes needed to drive the gin were furnished by the persons whose cotton was being baled. On occasion he was paid in cash for the use of his gin and at other times, when he did not keep the seed and his share of the ginned cotton, his patrons paid him in farm produce such as pork, corn, or fodder. The practice was so profitable for him that he continued it every year from 1850 until 1862, and in the course of that period wore out three gins. When he first began to operate Beaver Bend he hired white laborers to run his gin, but within a few years his slaves had learned the job and took it over. Under the supervision of the overseer it was their task to turn out clean bales, for the condition of the bales naturally determined to a great extent the classification of the cotton and the prices received for it in open market. Much of Davis' success as a planter was decided in the gin house and he, conscious of this fact, was also usually present to supervise the gin when it was in operation.

During his first years as a planter, Davis' cotton was floated by flatboat down the Cahaba to the Alabama River, thence from the town of Cahaba was shipped by river boat to Mobile. In 1851, however, in order to save on transportation costs he began hauling part of his staple in plantation wagons to Cahaba or Selma and then shipped it from one of those places down the Alabama River to market. From 1853 to 1855, wagons were used exclusively both for transporting cotton to the River and for bringing supplies back to the plantation. In the latter year wagons were deserted with the coming of the Cahaba and Marion Railroad to Hamburg, the little town near which Beaver Bend was located. This shift in method was made for obvious reasons. Davis was a stockholder in the railroad. Moreover, when wagons were run there was often a shortage of labor at the plantation.

Frequently the roads were impassable, and the railroad was a trust-worthy means of getting his bales to market when he wanted them there. With the Mobile market fluctuating as it normally did, the time of arrival of cotton there often meant rather large gains or losses for a planter, especially if he had instructed his factor to sell bales on arrival. In Davis' case, however, cotton was ordinarily stored to wait on a rise in prices. When he had employed flatboats to get his staple to Cahaba he was often held up for days because of low water in the Cahaba River, for at times the stream became so low that even small boats could not operate. Shipment was frequently uncertain. When wagons had been used he had trouble because of bad roads. He must have been greatly relieved when the opportunity came to use a railroad to ship his bales at least as far as the Alabama River. With few exceptions from September, 1855 until the Civil War, his shipments to Mobile were made by rail either to Cahaba, or to a little place known as Marion Junction located on the Cahaba and Marion Railroad, thence to Selma. From these points the staple was sent down the river to market. Still there were difficulties because facilities on the Alabama River itself were also frequently inadequate. It, too, became so low at times that boats could not operate. On a few occasions when this was the case Davis became so impatient to sell his cotton that he disposed of it in Selma rather than Mobile.

When cotton reached Mobile it came under the charge of a factor, and when Davis turned planter he had an immediate introduction to the established method of selling cotton. In his first month at Beaver Bend he was approached both by commission merchants who wished to arrange, at a 2½% commission, for his purchases of supplies and by factors who sought to handle, at the same commission, the sale of his cotton. A letter from one Mobilian, W. R. Brown, who was conducting both a commission house and a factorage business, is typical. On February 3, 1848, he obtained a supply of blacksmith tools for Davis, shipped them to him, and wrote that he could furnish any supply not obtainable in Perry County. He stated further that he was a factor, as well as the owner of a dry goods establishment, and requested that his name be mentioned to other planters in Perry County. He concluded, "If I can Serve you by attending to anything for you, Command me."

As it happens, Brown was not retained as factor and instead Davis gave his cotton business to a former Dallas County planter by the name of John R. Goree. At the time Goree was well liked by the planters around Beaver Bend and indeed had wide business connections in Perry County. The factor's family relations in Perry County are also worthy of note. He was the son-in-law of Edwin W. King, the second largest slave- and land-owner of the county, and especially because of this excellent connection he had a large clientele in the region. In addition to this, some of his own blood relatives in Dallas County were among Davis' closest friends. He had moreover had experience as a factor since the 1830's. For these reasons he was allowed to sell the Beaver Bend cotton during Davis' first four years as a planter. In 1852, Davis turned to W. M. Pleasant (later Gates and Pleasant) as his factor; and as far as is known all of the Beaver Bend cotton sold in Mobile between 1848 and 1862 was handled through these firms.

Davis' business relations and his correspondence with his Mobile factors form one of the most interesting phases of his career. Among the important functions of a factor was that of keeping his clients posted on market conditions and in this connection one of the first letters the new owner of Beaver Bend received from Goree is typical of many that followed. It was written on November 24, 1848: "We have had quite an animated market for three days past. Rates that had been refused were readily given—and large Sales effected— Middlings 4¾ to 4⅞. Good middlings 4⅞. Middler 5 to 5⅛ — fair 5¼. . . . I fear the consequences when the River gets up and large quantities arrive with its restless owners. If you have been here, at such times you know better than I can inform you." Such was Davis' introduction to the vicissitudes of the life of a planter—cotton selling at about five cents a pound when it was generally recognized that in order to make expenses a planter had to get at least eight cents! But he should perhaps have known that his new life would not be an easy one in every respect and that he would have to accept the bad with the good. Earlier in the year he was fore-warned what to expect when a friend in Mobile wrote, on June 7, that "I presume you will receive the bad news from France which reached Mobile yesterday, about as soon as you will receive this letter; so I will only say, cotton was reduced in price, one ¼ cent by the news received yesterday. No cotton selling at all, & would not command if sold more than 5¼ cts. So I was told last evening by a commission merchant." With conditions such as this in June he should not have been greatly surprised at the news received from Goree in November, although it is admitted that conditions could have changed for the better in the interval.

At the time of the receipt of Goree's letter, Davis had some cotton in Mobile ready for sale, but refused to accept what he considered such a miserable price for it. He seems to have made a decision here to wait out the market as long as possible in the hopes of a rise in price. It might be added that from this time on he consistently followed the practice of selling his cotton each year early in the market season, before large shipments were made to Mobile, or late in the season, when large portions of annual crops had been sold. Be that as it may, in December, 1848, the price for the best grade of cotton had risen only to 5¾ cents a pound, and Davis still refused to sell. He waited as long as he could, but finally in the first week of March, 1849, had to sell his 1848 crop because he had to meet payment on some of the due bills and drafts which had been given in his operation of the plantation since January, 1848. On March 12, he wrote in his farm book that "The cotton Crop of 1848—52 bales—was Sold by John R. Goree commission Merchant—12 March 1849, at 6¼ cents per pound—amounting to $1543.00." By holding out he had obtained a better price, but his proceeds were entirely inadequate to pay his first year's expenses. The main reason he could continue at Beaver Bend was the credit extended to him by his merchant friends in Marion. Fry, Bliss and Company, of Mobile, was not so lenient, however, and on April 7, 1849, wrote that "Our wants prompt us to ask an early remittance [of $109.77 for supplies purchased since November, 1848], as money is almost our only reliance, particularly as 19 twentieths of our purchases have to be made with cash." What was done about this request is unknown, although it is probable that the bill was paid with borrowed money.

Despite the low prices received for the 1848 crop, Davis continued with his waiting game when his 1849 crop had been prepared for sale. On December 5, he instructed Goree to hold his cotton until a certain price was reached. The exact price desired is unknown, but Goree's reply five days later was, "Your orders in reference to Cotton Shall be implicitly obeyed on its arrival." Since cotton at the time was selling at $9\frac{1}{2}$ to $10\frac{3}{4}$ cents it is obvious that Davis wanted more. A few days later, twenty-four Beaver Bend bales were in Goree's hands and cotton was still bringing from 10 to $10\frac{1}{8}$ cents a pound, but the factor informed his client, "I dont want to Sell till after the 1st January accounts [of prices being paid in England] are received." This again indicates that Davis wanted somewhat more than ten cents a pound for his cotton. He still withheld instructions to sell. That he was again wise in his speculations is shown by the prices finally obtained. On February 20, 1850, he recorded in his farm book: "This crop—1849—Sold by John R Goree—51 Bales @ $11\frac{1}{2}$ Feby 20— brought $2,889.00." Perhaps this time he obtained the price for which he had been waiting. At least he could feel elated over the outcome, for he had almost doubled his proceeds over the previous year despite having one less bale to sell. But if he could have waited a little longer he could have done even better, because on May 19 he received word that cotton was bringing twelve cents a pound. It is again probable, however, that he had to move his cotton in February in order to satisfy his creditors.

Of all the correspondence between Davis and his factor that concerning his 1850 crop is the most interesting and complete. It serves as a typical illustration of many of the relations between an Alabama planter and his Mobile factor. On November 7, shortly after the season had opened in Mobile, Goree wrote, "I am now at my post and take pleasure in communicating the news of our market. Cotton is in demand at $13\frac{1}{4}$ to $14\frac{1}{2}$c. Middling $13\frac{3}{4}$, full $\frac{3}{8}$ to $\frac{1}{2}$c above New Orleans—owing no doubt to our small stock. In Western Produce Prices are—Sugar 7 to 8. Coffee 13 to $14\frac{1}{2}$. Salt 125. Flour 6 to $6\frac{1}{2}$. Mess Pork $13. Bagging $14\frac{1}{2}$. Rope $7\frac{1}{2}$. The crop will reach according to late accounts 2250,000 Bales —Mobile receipts are now estimated 420 to 450,000." Davis was naturally encouraged at the receipt of such news and on the basis of it instructed Goree concerning the prices expected for his crop. The price must have been about fifteen cents a pound, for on January 11, 1851, Goree informed Davis, "Your minimum is a high price for the cotton now here. I hope the next [news from Europe] will improve it Enough to bring it up to yr. notch. Whenever it is obtained, or its advance, will uninstructed sell unless the light of a very heavy advance breaks on my vision—I am in the highest possible price for yours.

I would like to see your hat in hand—it would do me good among my friends in Perry. . . ." Such an optimistic outlook was perhaps justified at the time this letter was written, but Goree seems to have forgotten, at least temporarily, that many factors could cause the bottom to drop from the market at almost any time. Davis would have been wise in this particular case to sell as soon as his cotton got to market, but he held out for a rising price. On February 4 he was still speculating. Unfortunately for him, on that date Goree sent word that news had just been received on the English market which had reduced the price of middlings to 11¾c. The factor lamented, "Oh how that stings me," but always hopeful he added, "But hold up. I have confidence it will revive again. . . . I am holding on trying to Strengthen the market. The fourth is now over, and I think things will work better Soon. . . ."

Davis did not wish Goree to play with his cotton any longer and, needing cash money to make a payment on a note given in his purchase of Beaver Bend, he sent word to sell enough of his bales to bring twelve hundred dollars. Always the speculator, however, he qualified his instructions by stating that he would not sell for less than 12⅞c. If this price could not be reached he hoped that Goree could advance him the money and send it to Beaver Bend by one of his brothers-in-law, who at the time was in Mobile on business. The factor's reply, on February 14, was that the hoped for price could not be obtained, but "I send you the money by Mr. Jones—prices are low, Say 11 to 11⅛ for middlings. Please send me your note payable at 60 days—for the 1200 dollars." This letter finally convinced Davis that he was holding out for too much for his cotton and, on February 22, when he sent Goree his note for the twelve hundred dollars, he submitted new instructions about the sale of his cotton. Four days later the factor replied that thirty bales would be put up for sale and that he would "not turn away from 11¼c—to get 11½c will be out of the question unless things are a good deal better than they have been today. . . . Middlings today sold at 10⅛ to 10¼." Then the factor added a pertinent observation, "If we could get all hands to hold on two days and did not receive some additional very bad news from Europe we would see Middlings again at 11 to 11½c. But I fear the negro mania, pork mania, mule mania & land mania of Nov. & Dec. has drawn too many drafts to allow much to be held, that will sell at

10c. I am clinging on with a death grip—*hoping* some good news may arrive to keep us up until the receipts of our Ports fall off so rapidly as to convince John Bull, that the Crop is indeed a short one." The price Davis wanted, probably 11½c, could not be obtained and again he had to lower his demands. On March 20 he was seeking eleven cents, but even that could not be secured. Five days afterwards, Goree informed him that he was asking too much "and today the demand has been So limited that no brokers have been out." Unwelcomed reports from England had once more depressed the Mobile market. Still Goree remained undaunted, repeating his earlier belief that within a short time prices would rise again, just as soon as it was realized in England that receipts of cotton in Mobile were indeed falling off. "They are now retrograding every week and must convince John Bull, that our crop will not reach over 2250,000 Bales. This is the great point now on which the price depends. Dont be alarmed. As soon as your limit can be had, I will sell—11c is a fine price." The factor concluded his letter with an invitation to Davis to pay him a visit in Mobile, "if for nothing else at least to see how badly a great deal of cotton is ginned & picked." A few days later, on the last of the month, the factor finally sold the cotton about which such a lengthy correspondence had occurred. The whole lot, sixty-two bales, weighing 31,744 pounds, was sold at 10¾c a pound and brought $3,412.48. After deducting charges $209.07 for freight, wharfage, weighing, drayage, storage, and a commission of 2½%, Goree credited Davis' account with the sum of $3,203.41. On the same day an account current with the factorage house was forwarded to Beaver Bend:

1850
April 23 To Cash paid for copy Writ Ct. Court	$ 1.00
June 4 To Cash paid for Justice Fee	.25
Oct. 8 To Merchandise Bagg. & Rope deliv you by Lawsons	141.13
Oct. 8 To Interest on Same to March 31st	5.38
1851	
Jany 9 To Cash pd per yr Dft fav. A. C. Austin	236.04
Jany 9 To Interest on Same to March 31st	4.30
Feby 5 To Merchandise Plough Points Bill rend	1.50
Feby 14 To Cash Sent you by W. A. Jones	1,200.00
April 8 To Amt yr Note discounted due 30th inst	1,216.00
April 8 To Amt due you to Balance	1,611.27
	$4,416.87

1850
Oct. 8 By 1 Coil rope returned by you	$ 12.68
Oct. 8 By Interest on Same to March 31st	.12

1851
March 4 To Cash pro yr note discounted.............................. 1,200.66
March 31 To Cotton Sales rend..................................... 3,203.41

$4,416.87

This account current is of interest for several reasons. It indicates first that Davis' income from cotton sales increased slightly over the preceding year. The money which he had borrowed from Goree in February, 1850, had been used to make a payment on his land and the note of $1216.00, accepted by the factor in April, had been employed to make payment on slaves. Thus he was paying his debts. The relatively few purchases made through Goree's factorage house bears out the point earlier made that Davis secured most of his plantation supplies in Perry County. It will be noted, too, that there was an interest charge on every article purchased. The extended correspondence about the 1850 crop also deserves a few more words. Davis on his part had been obstinate and determined to hold out for a high price, so much so that he borrowed money to meet his engagements in the interval. But he procrastinated so long that at last he was caught short, and was finally forced to sell at a price lower than that which he could have obtained several times after his cotton had reached Mobile. As for Goree, the factor led Davis on with what might be described as over-confidence or an undue show of optimism. The final result of the correspondence and sale of the cotton was a strain on the cordial relations which had formerly existed between the two men. Davis seems to have blamed Goree for the outcome of his attempts at speculation. Goree no doubt held Davis responsible. Nevertheless, in 1851 Goree was allowed to sell the Beaver Bend cotton. No information is available on Davis' instructions to his factor about this crop, but at an early date in 1852 the crop "of 63 bales [115,624 pounds] was sold—56 [bales] @ 7¼—7 bales @ 6½—proceeds Net—$2,090.00." His reaction to such an unfortunate outcome may be well imagined. Be that as it may, he had been thinking of giving his business to a firm which handled both factorage and commission merchant affairs. Immediately after the sale of his 1851 crop he turned to the Mobile firm headed by W. M. Pleasant.

Presumably there was nothing unusual in the manner in which the 1852 cotton crop was disposed, other than that part of it was sold in Selma. It was at this period that Davis began selling portions of his crops in Selma, doing so because of bad roads between Beaver Bend

and Cahaba and also in order to save on costs of transportation to
Mobile. Possibly of equal importance was the fact that cotton sold
in the Dallas County town brought immediate cash. Regardless of
the reason, twelve bales of his 1852 crop were sold at the local market,
bringing 9½c a pound. Altogether, he made 117,412 pounds of seed
cotton and ginned a total of sixty-nine bales. There is no information
on his procedure in selling his fifty-seven bales in Mobile. It is established, however, that the last of his crop was sold in February, 1853,
and this seems to indicate that he again held on to his cotton as long
as possible in an effort to get a good price. The price obtained by
Pleasant amounted to 10¼c, which of course was quite an improvement over the preceding year.

In 1853, Davis was very definitely speculating again. In that year
he produced eighty bales, weighing 39,828 pounds, eight of which
were sold in Selma. On January 28, 1854, Pleasant wrote that fifty-
one bales had arrived in Mobile, "but will not nett your limit So I
will lay it aside to await the result of your speculation." Prices at the
time were going down and Davis was warned to expect them to go
still lower because of large receipts in the market town. In February,
the factor's prophecy was fulfilled and Davis held on to his bales
throughout the month. By March 14 prices had moved upwards
again, but still had not reached nine cents a pound. On that date,
Pleasant wrote that the last of the 1853 crop had been received and
that the shipment, too, had been "laid aside to abide the result of
your Speculation on time." Nothing has been learned about the final
prices received, but Davis must have been pleased with Pleasant because he continued to deal through him the next year.

Again in selling his 1854 bales Davis speculated. As reported by
Pleasant, on February 26, 1855, sixteen bales had been offered at eight
cents a pound, but "Buyers Say its too much price and leave before
conceding." Undaunted, Davis held on, but in April he had some
pressing obligations to meet and for the only time in his career as a
planter shipped a cargo of cotton to his factor accompanied by instructions "to Sell . . . as Soon as received at his option." This departure from his usual procedure must have been disappointing to
Davis, however, for when the next shipment of cotton was ready for
market it was sent to Selma for sale. On May 14, twenty-five bales
were sold there at 9¼c, bringing in $1,064.00. A few days later, W.

M. Pleasant turned up at Beaver Bend, probably to find out why the plantation had not been sending its usual number of bales to Mobile. Despite the arguments the factor must have given concerning the advantages of the Mobile market over Selma, twenty additional bales from the plantation were sold in the latter place a few days after Pleasant's departure. Fourteen bales brought 10c and six bales brought 9c a pound. Thus of the total of seventy-nine bales made in 1854, forty-five—more than half of them—were sold in Selma. The next year, however, Davis once more shipped most of his bales to Mobile and, as had become his established practice, tried once more to hold on to it and to out-figure the market. On March 17, 1856, he had eighteen bales at market for which he was asking 10c a pound. Gates and Pleasant, which had become the firm name of the outfit formerly headed by Pleasant, informed him that the bales were not first-rate and would "not Command more than 8 to 8¼ Cents. Two would Command 9 cents. . . ." Demand for cotton was good and it was hoped that soon the price would rise. On the basis of this information and also because his figure could not be reached, Davis decided to hold off until a later date. This time his waiting game proved of some value, for his eighteen bales were sold on May 6 and brought 9⅛c a pound. Even so, he did not get the ten cents he had asked for at first. Altogether he made seventy-seven bales in 1855. Besides the above eighteen sold in Mobile, thirty-nine others were sold there at 9c. Twenty bales were disposed of at 8¾c in Selma.

His correspondence about his 1856 crop is the last group of business letters which has been located. The market season started out with prospects of good prices and he became quite excited over it. On September 27, he wrote in his farm book that "I think the prospect for a big price—say 12½ cents or the rise is increasing," and he determined at this time to play the market again for all it was worth. It is probable, too, that he set approximately twelve to thirteen cents a pound as the minimum to be accepted. On November 18, Gates and Pleasant informed him that thirty-two bales, middling to good middling cotton, had been received in Mobile and had been "laid aside until prices reach your figure or limit is removed." The highest price being offered for good middlings at the time was 11¾c, thus indicating that more than that sum was wanted. But Davis was unwilling to let his cotton go at the price and advised his factors to keep it in storage, for he was confident that at least 12c or 12½c would soon be reached. His excellent spirits are perhaps best indicated by an entry made in his farm book on December 31: "The year is ended— . . . like all former years it has come with good & evil fortune to the children of men. In our little home Circle—we have had more good than evil— . . . all in good health—good houses to Shelter us, good fires to warm us & good Clothes to hide our uncomely parts—Our Corn is plentiful, our meat nearly so—Our Cotton above average and Selling high— . . . Our flocks are in good order & all things Conspire to fill our hearts with gratitude to the Giver of all good."

On January 24, 1857, Davis was still asking more for his cotton than was being paid in open market, being informed by his factors that "We are offering 11 bales @ 12½ but Cannot yet obtain it." Word was sent also, however, that "The last accounts from Liverpool rec'd this morning Shows an improvement in that Market yet no effect has been produced here." A few days later another letter, dated January 28, was received at Beaver Bend. It is quoted at length because it affords additional information upon Davis' plan of selling his 1856 crop and also upon the honesty of his factor. The effect which the condition of the cotton market in England could have on the market in Mobile is also mentioned:

Sometime Since you directed us to Sell the first Shipment on hand . . . if 12½ and upwards Could be obtained, and hold the balance for the Spring Market. Early this morning by accident 11 bales was Sold at 12¼ Cents. . . . Should that Style Cotton advance to that figure [12½c] we are bound to you for the additional ¼ Cent. The Cotton Can now be replaced at a little less than the price obtained as we have received this evening news of 1/6 d. decline in Liverpool. This morning after Stating the Condition of the Cotton [that is, Davis' instructions about selling it] to the Broker, he would not let us off. Now is quite willing. Our object is Simply to know if you would rather now accept the Sale, and in that decision we ask that it be made without reference to our interests or wishes. We hope to hear from you Soon.

As will be shown later, Davis allowed this sale to stand and was reimbursed for his loss. The accident was admittedly the fault of the factors and they took their loss gracefully. As a matter of fact, only two days after the incident occurred they wrote Davis a letter offering to extend him a large amount of credit. Earlier, on September 24, 1856, the master of Beaver Bend had purchased four slaves costing him $4,050. At that time he had prospects of an excellent crop and as he indicated in his farm book a few days later he expected cotton to bring at least 12½c a pound. Such a situation was too tempting and, just as most planters did under such circumstances, he bought his four additional slaves. On January 1, 1857, he obtained a Negro man for $1,250. Then, on January 9, he signed drafts of $4,050 in payment of the four negroes, and a few days later inquired of Gates and Pleasant if they would help out in the purchase of the Negro man. On January 30, the factors replied with a most interesting letter, one which furnishes more information on the functions of a factor and in this case shows the trust Davis' agents placed in him. This letter, too, is quoted at length because of the significant material it contains:

In regard to your Drfts for the purchase of Negroes We have to Say that we want to aid you as much as we can—are willing that your Cash indebtedness to us, after Sale of your Cotton, Shall be $3000, and Should you need more We Suggest however that in your purchases you could do quite as Well by giving Bills on us maturing next fall on which there would be no charge by us, and which you would not be required to meet until Such time as might be convenient to get your Crop to market, because we would pay them. In this arrangement the only difference would be that you would pay interest to the holder of the bill instead of to us. If however this suggest. do not appear feasible or practicable with your Views—then draw at 10 or 15 days Sight giving us notice.

On the basis of this promise, Davis signed a draft in payment of his Negro man and it is probable that one or two more were purchased, for on February 17 his factors wrote: "We fear that our Suggestions with Reference to Drafts was not as well defined as they ought to have been—We meant to be understood that if you Could make the Same trade on time with interest added as for Sight paper—we would prefer. We did not intend to thwart your purposes, but enough— We hope We are understood. Your paper will be honored." Afterwards, Davis held on to his cotton until March 5. On that date he recorded in his farm book that he had sold "8 Bales @ 12½, 32 @ 12c, 11 @ 12½c, 4 @ 14c, 20 @ 13c—The best sales by far I ever made."

In succeeding years Davis continued his practice of trying to beat the market, and in his speculating usually planned out his campaign at the beginning of the selling season in Mobile. Ordinarily he endeavoured to ship some of his crop to market early in the season in order to obtain the good prices being offered then. Other portions of crops were sent to market late in the season to take advantage of the better prices which were customarily offered in the spring. In addition, he kept some bales in storage in Mobile, to be sold when and

if there occurred a sharp upturn in the market. The cotton of course
was not sold until a certain minimum, decided upon by Davis, was
reached. In other words, in selling his cotton he used his head. For
example, on November 16, 1857, he stated, "My object is to Sell 30
bales at present prices, say 12 to 12½ & hold the residue for 60 days—
& then Sell 30 more—we now have 72 which will equal in weight 78
Bales of 500 lbs." This plan looked beautiful on paper, but as may
always be expected in selling cotton unforeseen factors may develop
which cause the best laid plans to go haywire. Such was the case on
this occasion.

As it has so often happened, unsettled financial affairs in Europe
shortly afterwards caused the bottom to drop out of the cotton markets
in the United States. This time it was the temporary suspension of
specie payment by the Bank of England. On November 26, Davis
had heard "of Cotton falling 4 cents!!" If all his sales of the 1857
crop were as bad as the one about which information is available, he
had a miserable year after the successes of 1856. On February 4,
1858, he sold some of his bales in Selma and had to accept slightly
less than ten cents a pound. Such a turn of events was unfortunate
for him because his 1857 crop was the largest produced at Beaver
Bend to that date. The slaves picked out 211,572 pounds, or approximately 115 bales. Despite the outcome, in the next year he
turned up with a more complete plan than ever before for selling
his crop. On October 30, 1858, he wrote in his farm book, "My plan
of Selling my crop as far as matured is to Sell 40 Bales in Novr—40
in Decr—40 in March & 20 in June—1st 11⅝c—2nd at 12 & 3rd
12½ & 4th at 13." The outcome of this plan is unknown, although
part of it must have been executed because cotton was being shipped
to Mobile as late as April 14, 1859.

The 1858 crop was the biggest yet, amounting to 245,258 pounds
of raw cotton, or 154 bales. Since it is known that prices of the
previous year were maintained, it is assumed that at least ten cents a
pound must have been received. Production the next year was still
better, resulting in the largest output in any year at the plantation.
Seed cotton weighing 284,881 pounds was picked. When ginned this
aggregate made 196 bales weighting 94,497 pounds. The 1860 crop
fell off to 253,314 pounds of raw cotton, mainly because acreage was
lowered from 380 in 1859 to 290 in 1860. The 1861 acreage was

pushed back up to 325 acres, but in that year, partially because of the vicissitudes of the first year of the Civil War and also because of Davis' invalidism, Beaver Bend produced only 151,028 pounds. It will be remembered, too, that overseer troubles also cut down output.

Now there arises a question that has intrigued students of Southern history for a long time. Was it profitable to operate a cotton plantation in the Deep South in the ante-bellum period? Some modern scholars say no, a minority say yes. For many years all Lower South cotton planters of the period before 1861 were popularly believed to have been successful nabobs, graciously managing their self-sufficient, extensive agricultural establishments. The plantation system was looked upon as a sort of lost paradise, or perhaps as a Southern version of Shangri-la. Those families whose property had been lost helped this conception along considerably. Stories told by ex-slaves also added luster to descriptions handed down about the old days. Then came modern scholarship with its impertinent habit of refuting many established beliefs. First there was a scientific inquiry into slavery as a whole, the system was studied beautifully, broken down into its various elements, and suggestions made that it was quite unprofitable. Next came investigations of the activities of the Southern planter and slave-owner in particular states. This time it was stated emphatically and figures were called upon to indicate that the peculiar institution, as practiced in specific states, was not an economic success. Now, some historians, dissatisfied with the whole problem, have come finally to the conclusion that the presentation of the subject has been too impersonal and that perhaps there is still too much generalization. The result has been more detailed studies of the individual planter, with the hope that at least the questions of the profitability, self-sufficiency, and other features of the plantation system in his case may be answered at last. All this may lead to more confusion than ever before, for after enough of the detailed studies are completed writers will then come forward to synthesize the works of their colleagues. Then what shall we have but the conclusion that the whole system of plantation management was one of degree, that profits were difficult and even impossible to determine at times, and that the success or failure of a plantation often depended to a large extent on the personal characteristics and energy of its owner? There is no question that many planters made profits. Some produced large amounts of staple crops, sold them at opportune times, while others were not so fortunate. All planters had to purchase certain of their necessities. Some succeeded, others failed.

What about Davis? Of importance is the fact that his records are incomplete. His farm books and correspondence nowhere indicate the prices received for cotton made at Beaver Bend during his last years at the plantation. It can only be assumed that as a result of the average price of eight to ten cents a pound paid for cotton in Mobile in those years and because of his established system of waiting for good prices he must have obtained at least ten cents per pound for the staple. It might be added, too, that in his last seven years at Beaver Bend he happened to be in the planting business at one of the periods of greatest profit for planters in his state. His years of least profit were of course during the first part of his residence at Beaver Bend, at a time when he was paying for his land, buying slaves, clearing land, ditching, buying supplies, and making general improvements. He started from scratch in 1848—at his death in 1862 he was a man of wealth. Some of that wealth came from his law practice, a small portion came from sale of property owned in Marion and elsewhere, and his wife inherited a few slaves from her father. Despite these added sources of income, he must be considered as a successful planter.

It is difficult to determine Davis' exact wealth in 1862, because the Civil War had already brought some inflation, although the height of inflation had certainly not been reached as early as 1862. Even so, his wealth was tangible enough, as witnessed by the action of the Perry County Probate Court on January 3, 1863, when the executors of Davis' will were ordered to file bonds for the total sum of $240,-000.[2] On January 12, when his estate was appraised it consisted of: 5,138 acres of farm land, and eleven town lots in Marion; seventy-eight slaves, valued at $63,965; stock, including horses, mules, hogs, cows, bulls, oxen, sheep and goats, at $5,152; farm implements and equipment, $1,771; farm produce on hand, consisting of corn, fodder, peas, potatoes, salt pork, salt, linseed oil and rough wool, at $14,524; household goods, including a library of 631 volumes, $2,379.25; and notes owed to the estate, $2,947.32.[3] This was his property, represent-

[2]Perry County, Minutes, Probate Court (Office of Probate Court, Courthouse, Marion), K, 67, 68.
[3]Jordan, " 'System of Farming at Beaver Bend,' Alabama, 1862," *loc. cit.*, VIII, 77.

ing the results of fourteen and a half years as owner and operator of Beaver Bend. For an equal number of years he had previously practiced law. All available records show, however, that most of his holdings were obtained, that is, paid for after the year 1848, at which time he turned to planting as a career. Hugh Davis was one Deep South planter who was a success. For him plantation slavery was profitable. Now the question is: How was his estate affected by the Civil War and the chaos which followed?

_____ 8

BEAVER BEND DURING THE CIVIL WAR
AND AFTERWARDS

THERE IS NO QUESTION that the Civil War and its aftermath ruined the plantation system in Alabama as practiced in the ante-bellum period. The case of Beaver Bend was no different from all the other agricultural establishments in the state, for it, too, was changed drastically by the events between 1861 and 1876. When the War came the plantation was at last approaching self-sufficiency, the land comprising the place was bought and paid for, no debts were owed on slaves or other property, and cotton was bringing good prices. Eighteen large fields at the place had been cleared and were under cultivation. Hugh Davis, Sr., with his long and effective experience as a planter, had learned how to manage his establishment, the slaves were working acceptably, and output of all produce was steadily increasing. The point had just been reached when even greater returns could be expected from the work and expense involved in opening up and developing the plantation. All this, however, was interrupted by the War, with its horror, disruption of ordinary activities, inflation, loss of markets for cotton, and new social, economic, and political conditions. By the end of the conflict Beaver Bend had changed so radically that it could scarcely be recognized as the same place. New methods of management had necessarily been adopted, slave labor was replaced with free share-croppers (whites and Negroes), and a new generation of Davises was in control. Nevertheless, the members of the family had managed to hold on to their land and after the War they stayed with it.

In general charge of the plantation during the harsh Civil War years was Lewis C. Tutt, a lawyer and banker of Marion, who had married one of the elder Davis' sisters-in-law. As provided by Davis' will, Tutt became administrator of the estate in June, 1862. He continued in that capacity until December, 1869.[1] When the War began, Hugh Davis, Jr., aged eighteen, and his brother, Albert, aged sixteen, were enrolled in the University of Alabama at Tuscaloosa, and along with a majority of the student body there they immediately entered the Army. Throughout most of the War they were in the field. Left in Marion, when the struggle started, were the invalided Hugh Davis, Sr; his wife; Sarah Matilda, aged thirteen; and Nathaniel, four years old. Until June, 1862, the elder Davis sent out orders to his overseer at Beaver Bend; afterwards Tutt acted as absentee-superintendent. In actual charge of the plantation in the spring of 1861 was an old man named J. B. Clay, who had become overseer in April, when his predecessor left to join the fighting forces. Clay remained at the place until July 18, 1864, when he, too, quit his job to enter the fight. At intervals Hugh, Jr., obtained furloughs from his command to come home and help out. Throughout the summer of 1864 he was on leave of absence because of a severe leg wound, and managed Beaver Bend until he had to return to the field on August 25. From September 1 until the end of the year an overseer named W. I. Howell was in charge of the plantation. For some reason Howell quit his job on January 1, 1865, and from that time until the close of the War activities were supervised by an overseer named Gates. It was under the direction of these various persons that the effort was made during the War to manage the property which the elder Davis bequeathed to his family.

In the War years the Davises of course did not fare as well as in the ante-bellum period, and, like others, they had to turn for the most part to a pay-as-you-go system. The easy credit of the late fifties was gone. Even so, the plantation managed to turn out some produce for sale and the family usually had money which was required for the

---

[1]Perry County, Will Book, III, 306-311; Perry County, Probate Court, Minutes, M, 552 (Office of Probate Court, Marion).

purchase of many of its needed supplies, that is, for those necessities which were available. Fortunately, there is extant an account of the total receipts and expenditures of the Davis estate from June, 1862 to August 15, 1865. Tutt, as administrator, was required by law to maintain such a record of his management of funds, and thus it is known that in the last three years of the War the family had in its hands an average of slightly more than seven thousand dollars cash annually. Undetermined portions of the income were derived from rents of property in Marion, while cotton sales brought in the sum of $13,379.00. The years in which the bales were made is unknown, however. Beaver Bend's expert Negro carpenter, Wright, was hired out frequently and for his work the family received a sum of $388.73. Farm produce in large quantities was sold in open market in Marion and Selma, and from all sources the estate received $22,821.41 in cash between June 28, 1862 and August 15, 1865. Under pre-War conditions such a sum would have been quite ample to maintain the family and Beaver Bend for a period of three years, but with War prices on the increase, especially after 1861, the Davises and all others in the South were compelled to change their ways of living. Exact individual expenditures are unknown, although practically all of the income was spent. Even calico got as high as fifteen dollars a yard in Marion during the War. Annual expenditures each year were as follows: $693.00 in 1862; $1,053.53 in 1863; $20,094.35 in 1864; and $980.53 in the first three months of 1865. The War thus drained the family of all its cash resources by the end of 1864. Such was the case with other families in the region. Cash assets of the Davises amounted to $15.67 between March and August, 1865.[2] Conditions would have been much worse, however, if the Davises had not had their plantation to help carry them through the ordeal. At least they still had their land.

Management of Beaver Bend under war conditions was as good as could be expected. J. B. Clay, who worked as overseer for more than three years of the period, was conscientious and hard-working in most respects. In general, routine work was performed in much the same fashion as under his predecessors and with the advice of Tutt he tried to the best of his ability to carry on. His one great fault was failure to keep a complete record of his work. Most of his entries in the

[2]Perry County, Inventory of Estates (Office of Probate Court, Marion), M, 138-142.

farm books had only to do with weather conditions and never was an entry made without some mention of the matter. Even some of those entries are worth quoting, however, for the quaint manner of writing which the man employed. On February 15, 1862, he recorded, "This hes been the worst day that we hev had this winter hit hes been Sleten and Snowen and rainen all day maken cloes Shucken and Shelen Corn grinden worken on the rode worken in Shop." On December 25, 1862, he wrote, "this is Chrismas morning and abutiful morning it is we shud be thankful to god that we hev lived to See the sun rise one moer Chrismas and if we shood live to see anuther may we live moer devoted to his care all is well." It was recorded, March 12, 1863, "we had Astrom on last Sunday night that blue dawn lotes of timbar." He indicated, on December 7, 1863, "This is a nise warm shun shina day the first we heve had in aweak." These entries are typical. Be that as it may, Clay was a faithful worker and was largely responsible for holding Beaver Bend together during a great part of the War. Because of exorbitant prices of all supplies and articles in the war period he was compelled to cut outlays of cash to the minimum. As a result, subsistence farming became of more importance than ever before, for great attention had to be given to the production of food-stuffs and other necessities if the people at the plantation hoped to survive.

Since there was a gradually tightening market during the war, cotton became of less importance to the producer than at any time in the whole nineteenth century. The 1861 crop amounted to 100,000 pounds less than the preceding year, the overseer reporting on October 26 that "The Coten the rotenies that I ever pick." The next year the output was so short that Hugh, on a visit at the time, wrote on November 28, "Finished picking cotton—this is one year it hasn't taken thirteen months in a year to gather a cotton crop." Only thirteen bales were made in 1863. In 1864 an all-time low was reached. Only twenty-three days were necessary to pick the miserable crop and the small amount of 15,314 pounds of raw cotton, about ten bales, were made. The staple brought $2,542.60 in 1862; sixteen bales, three of which had been held over from the preceding year, were sold in 1863 for $5,289.70; and twenty-three bales, made in the 1863 and 1864 seasons, were sold for $5,546.70 on February 28, 1865.

Effort and energy which formerly went into making a crop of the white staple was diverted during the War to production of food. There were few holidays, even at Christmas seasons. But despite great attention to the matter of cultivating food crops there was never enough to eat, and especially during the last two years of the War the Davis slaves were on short rations. As already mentioned, even in 1859 and 1860, when more foodstuffs were made than in any of the ante-bellum years, the elder Davis had had to purchase many articles. The seriousness of supplying adequate food for eighty people in the War years becomes still more apparent when it is remembered that domestic production had to suffice. No longer could it be easily supplemented. Meat produced each year never lasted until the next killing and even as early as November 28, 1862, it was reported that "the smoke house was empty." When hogs were killed the next month, 9,302 pounds were made, but this could not be expected to last out the year. More than twelve thousand pounds had been killed in 1859, and in the next year it had been necessary to purchase more than two thousand pounds. Therefore, the 1862 killings were quite inadequate. Production was still shorter the next year, and from 1863 onward the Negroes were usually on a very short meat ration. Pork's place in the diet was taken by roasting ears, peas, and green vegetables. Unwittingly, however, as will be shown later, the Federal Army helped out on this score in the spring of 1864 when a Northern drive into Mississippi caused Southern officials to drive thousands of hogs from that state into Alabama in order to prevent their confiscation by the conquerors. Many of the hogs were driven into Perry County and were killed on shares by local planters. For Beaver Bend this incident resulted in a gift of more than two thousand pounds of meat. Although pork for Negroes was usually scarce at the plantation during the War there was a more ample supply of vegetables. Grown every year were corn, peas, turnips, collards, cabbages, beans, and peanuts. Potatoes and rice in large quantities were cultivated. Also grown, but unsuccessfully, were wheat, rye, and millet. Now indeed it was necessary "to buy neither bread nor meat nor anything that can be made on the place." In 1862, a sugar mill was constructed and from it came many gallons of syrup from a new Beaver Bend crop, sugar cane. Dried fruits in larger quantities than ever before were put up for winter use. Vinegar was another article made at home.

Aside from food, one of the serious problems at the plantation in the War was provision of proper physical care for the Negroes. It was impossible to clothe them in the manner to which they were accustomed, but efforts were made to distribute minimum necessities throughout the struggle. Looms and spinning wheels were run full-time and rarely was a piece of cloth purchased. At no time during the War did a Beaver Bend Negro receive a pair of ready-made shoes, and after 1862 they wore shoes made of raw hide uppers and wooden bottoms. Housing facilities were adequate, but few repairs on cabins were made. Only on one occasion, moreover, was lime spread under the slave quarters. The outcome of this neglect was a greater amount of sickness among the Negroes and as might be expected the time lost from work because of illness increased appreciably over that lost before 1861. A limited diet enhanced the possibility of maladies of all sorts and it was impossible to obtain medicines with which to treat Negroes after they became ill. In the fall of 1861 there was a great amount of dysentery not only at Beaver Bend but throughout Perry County. At one time in the next summer ten Davis slaves were ill with chills, while others were down with bilious fevers, sore feet, and bone felons. Throughout the summer of 1863, at least ten Negroes were sick nearly every day. The next year while Hugh, Jr., was acting as supervisor of the plantation there was an undue amount of ailments, but being of the opinion that the Negroes were not so much indisposed as lazy the young Davis put all of them to work. In September, when he returned to the Army, sicknesses of many kinds broke out again, and from that time until the close of the War it was impossible at any time to put a full force to work in the fields. The slaves may have been lying down on their jobs, but undoubtedly there was more illness than in the ante-bellum years.

Another important cause of a reduction in the net output of the plantation during the War was the demands placed on all planters by government authorities. Both Alabama and the Confederacy were incessant in requests and orders for foodstuffs and plantation implements. Impressments were not infrequent. In addition, many of the Beaver Bend slaves were called at various times to work for either the state or central government. Even while at the plantation they were often forced to shell corn or prepare food for soldiers or government stock in the region. Droves of government animals being driven through the neighborhood were fed on local grainstuffs, and on several occasions all of the Davis slaves were put to sawing lumber for Army use. In 1863, a large portion of the men were sent to Selma to work on fortifications which were then being thrown up around that town. In other instances some of the hands were sent to Mobile for the same purpose. Their absences naturally interrupted ordinary work at the plantation and retarded production. But of greater significance in reducing net production were the various taxes in kind which had to be paid both to Alabama and Confederate governments. A soldier's general tax and an income tax in money were also paid. Produce appropriated by the Armies included meal, flour, bacon, beef, corn, fodder, hay, wheat, oats, buckwheat, rice, potatoes, syrup, peas, beans, and peanuts. Commissary Departments collected such articles as axes, spades, picks, crosscut saws, chisels, augurs, sets of harness, and log chains. In order better to conduct these impressments Alabama was divided along lines of its congressional districts, each district was subdivided into sections, and in each section certain localities or towns were designated as points of deposit or depots. On the basis of available records, it seems that the Davises and their neighbors gave up thousands of dollars worth of plantation supplies, produce, and implements.

The most interesting reports of affairs at Beaver Bend during the War were made by Hugh Davis, Jr. He can not be considered as the most important manager of the plantation because he was there infrequently, but at the same time his descriptions of activities when he was present are worthy of special notice. In 1864, in particular, he was engaged in directing the work of the plantation. An entry made in the farm book on March 9 is both significant and interesting:

Ma and I came down this morning—Found several of the best hands complaining but not much sick—They have showed their hoggish instinct in eating so much meat and grease that their digestive organs refuse to work well. Their bellies being overloaded have stalled—Dill has been applied to their machinery and will doubtless set them to going in a few days. . . . The recent raid of Gen. Sherman in Miss. caused the Quartermaster to drive a great number of hogs from that state to this—several thousand were brought to this neighborhood—and slaughtered and salted away, by the farmers, on shares—the farmers taking the pate, back bone, spare ribs, haslets & feet— We have fed away our little corn to the drove and killed 115—Made by the operation about two thousand pounds of meat which is a great addition to our short meat crop— Will kill some 50 more the first favorable spell of weather—The negroes have saved the entrails for soap grease, mixed with a little lye and boiled they will make a fine scavenger for their *ebony* bellies—All things are busy preparing for the coming crop. Overseer has most of the land ready to receive the seed—& some corn planted—Beaver Bend will turn out a good crop if her rugged bosom is only properly nourished—Have seen the pigs of which there are a goodly number and in fine order—Sheep and goats look well and increasing—

The loom and spinning wheel are busy—the *busing* of the wheels and the *him him* of the looms can be heard all day. We are almost independent of Yankee goods but not quite.

'Tis raining and the heavy clouds indicate a continuance—Ma will have a disagreeable drive home but it will not be of much consequence to a soldier nearly three years old—His eyes are open and have seen the Elephant—Bad weather is nothing to him.

My wound, received at Missionary Ridge is doing well—has not quite healed—a large scar is being left—leg not straight but I can get foot to ground—am hobbling on crutches—they are a great invention but a poor substitute for a leg—The M. Board has extended my leave of Absence for sixty days, that is, from the 8th inst. At the expiration of that time I hope to be able to return to the field and if fortune favors will revenge myself ten fold—Revenge is sweet and I will have it—Old Book! good bye until another time and then if I am alive my life continues—amen—Hugh Davis.

Following the above account, Hugh Davis returned to Marion and it was about two months before he entered in the farm book another account of affairs at the plantation. On May 11, in the manner of an army officer making a report to his commanding officer, he wrote to his overseer:

Arms of all kinds & calibre in good order except the *rod of correction* which could be improved by *use*. Ration of meat small but sufficient for the year—the Commissary Department otherwise well supplied—86 hogs, 32 Goats, 35 Sheep, 32 Beeves & milch cows—40 Turkeys—300 Chickens on hand—Quartermaster Dpt deficient in transportation—otherwise well supplied. Reveille—rather late and is doubtful whether the Captain [overseer] attends roll call—The engineer department has selected a good position and have fortified it well against any attack that Genl Starvation may make and I believe by the assistance of Providence that a victory can easily be gained. . . . Barrack sufficient and in good order—Some new and stringent orders would be of benefit especially an order calling the attention of the Captain to Gen orders [rules and regulations] from Head Qtrs. . . . I have the honor to be, Genl. Very Respectfully Your Obt Ser. Hugh Davis 2d Lt.

Later in the month, on May 28, Hugh reported again, this time recording that the corn was growing well, but that cotton was "very small for this season of the year." Potatoes, sugar cane, and millet were "doing well." Peas were indifferent. Cows were giving quantities of milk, but most of the pigs had died of cholera. Indeed, as stated by overseer Clay on March 20, the hogs had been "dying with callary." Altogether sixty-three pigs and hogs had died of the disease.

On July 18, when Clay left for the Army, Hugh moved out to Beaver Bend and took over active control until his own leave of absence expired, stating that "Though the drive is short still I hope it may be sweet & fast." He found corn and peas in excellent condition, that hogs were in "good order." It was added, however, that "The plantation, though, is not in good order there being many washes through the fields and about the hill—fences out of repair. Gates do. Cabbin lot and yard need policing badly—manure scattered and no pens to put it in. I might sum up by saying the big things are straight but the little ones crooked. I find 17 ploughs running and 16 hoes chopping." Immediately he began to set affairs straight. Large amounts of trash were hauled from the cabin lot. Tires were put on wheels of carts and wagons. The sugar mill was repaired. New gates and gate posts were built and old ones repaired. By the end of July he had finished hoeing, ploughing and laying by corn, cotton, and peas. Only potatoes were left to work and they were finished before the middle of August.

On August 25, Hugh left Beaver Bend to return to his command near Atlanta, Georgia, but before leaving pulled nearly all of the plantation fodder and put up sixty hogs to fatten for the following winter's killing. At the time of his departure, he explained, "I have Solomon foreman of the place. Johnson and Dick leaders of the plough & hoe hands respectively." Under the leadership of these Negroes, taking their orders from administrator Tutt, the plantation was operated until September 1. On the latter date, however, a white overseer named W. I. Howell was obtained, and as he described his arrangements, "Came here & set in on the first of Sept to attend to the business of the farm of the Est of Hugh Davis for which the Executors promise to pay me seventy five dollars at the end of the month or at such rate until I set in fer another period of time." Howell remained at Beaver Bend until the end of the year, employing most of his time in manufacturing cane syrup. He had such success with this task that he was able to barter some of it for bacon, wheat, and other foods.

There is no information available on the affairs at the plantation from the last of 1864 until May 18, 1865, except that the place was supervised by a man named Gates who succeeded Howell. The next bit of information comes from a lengthy entry made in the farm book on May 18, 1865, after Hugh, Jr., returned from the Wars. The entry is quoted in its entirety both for its descriptive powers and its account of conditions at Beaver Bend at the close of the Civil War. It furnishes a foretaste, too, of changing conditions:

Many and great changes have taken place since I have written in this book. Mr. Gates has been acting as overseer—came here and entered his duties 1st January 1865—Was discharged on 15th [May]—not from any fault of his but because of great political changes in Civil and military affairs—The federal Yanks stormed and captured Selma about 1st April and have occupied the city since—This department has been surrendered to the United States authorities—Orders have been issued vouchsafing freedom to negroes and they have all become monomaniacs on the subject of freedom—As soon as the order was issued thousands of them flocked to Selma to be free, to embrace the *nigger lovers*—Poor deluded creatures, they thought when they had crossed the breastworks around Selma they would be baptised with freedom and have nothing to do the rest of their lives but to kick up their heels and lay in the sunshine and work or not just as they pleased—Fond delusion! It soon passed away and they are *nearly all* at their homes at work. Freedom nor the accursed Yankees were not exactly what they had supposed them to be—They now know they must work for a living—George was the first of my negroes to runaway from home and go to the Yanks—d—n them, but he has found that 'home is the best place in the world.' Joe and Wright were next. Hanover soon followed—Says that he went off that he might marry one of Dr. Robbins negroes—they are living in Selma. On the 14th inst. seeing the negroes were all crazy to see the Elephant—I gave them passes and sent them to Selma telling them never to return but all did return except two—Hester and Amealia—Henrietta left this morning and Lucie, Solomon's wife, I understand will leave tonight. Joy go with them but if this military order, unconstitutional as it is, does not protect them always, all who have left or leave had better look out for I have a settlement with them all my own way too.

After this outburst, Davis added that thirteen men and thirteen women had "agreed to remain at home and work as they have heretofore done and to receive 1/5 of the growing crop of cotton, corn and potatoes and to be provisioned as compensation for their labor." He was thus rushing directly to the share-crop system.

For the next five months Hugh remained at the plantation, finding that because of disruptions of labor at the time of peace his crops were failing. On May 29, he "Commenced cutting wheat," but complained that it was "hardly worth the cutting." The next day, in disgust, he quit harvesting the crop and turned his stock into the fields. In June, he admitted that corn was growing fast, but stated also that it was no good and that grass was growing faster. Shortly afterwards, excessive rains came, caused the corn to tassle prematurely and ruined the crop. His fodder amounted to only thirty-three small stacks, few of which were worth saving. It was almost impossible to obtain ready cash and in order to raise some money Davis rented several of his plantation wagons and mules to cotton speculators who were hauling cotton out of Perry County. Even this venture turned out badly and as reported on August 29, Beaver Bend teams "were hardly [in] serviceable condition from bad treatment & neglect while hauling speculators' cotton—such as sore shoulders—2's hind legs badly sprained— one mule lost & 2 one eye put out." All these conditions were awful enough, but none was more serious than the problem of labor. Some of the hired hands left the plantation in May and several of those who remained failed to perform their jobs as they had promised in their contracts. Davis was a martinet, however, and every time a hand refused to execute orders a fine was imposed. The Negroes became so lax that a white man named Ellis was brought in to cut wheat, being paid one bushel per day for his work. On May 30, Hugh expressed the opinion that "Negroes will not work for pay, the *lash* is all I fear that will make them—I predict that since slavery has been abolished they will be a nuisance to the country; that very little cotton will be made hereafter." He added, "Nine good hands have deserted; may they reap the reward."

His troubles with freedmen continued in June, and on the first of the month five more hands quit the plantation. Included in the group was a Negro named Alex, who left his mother, wife, and two children at Beaver Bend. None of the family which remained were prime hands and not wishing to feed them they were immediately sent to join Alex, "wherever he may be." The white, Ellis, had turned out to be such a good worker, however, that he was retained as a sort of manager. On June 2 an agreement was made by which he was to continue at the plantation until the end of the year, his main job being to attend to the stock and keep the corn cribs locked "day and night." His pay was to consist of seventy bushels of corn and one hundred pounds of cotton, and he was to be provided with a house, three and one-half pounds of meat and one peck of meal each week. In addition, his children were to receive one peck of meal every week. On June 5, Davis "Hired 8 negro men to work six weeks for their victuals." But problems continued and three days later Davis fussed, "No Rain since 14th May, land very thirsty and crop suffering very much for rain—Grass growing rapidly in young corn—Seventeen of my best hands left home and gone to Selma—this leaves only a weak force to contend against 250 acres of grass—Two of the hired 'freedmen' have deserted, one carried [stole] the rations belonging to the others. . . . How lazily free negroes work. O for the use of the lash." A few days later several other freedmen were taken on for six weeks, this time for their food and eight bushels of corn each. Some of these also soon went away. Throughout the summer and fall of 1865 it was impossible to keep a working force, for no sooner were Negroes hired than they or others quit their jobs. Finally, in disgust, young Hugh also quit the plantation, moved to Marion, and resided there for the rest of his life. On October 3, 1865, he wrote: "Farewell Old Farm Book! to record the future work of free negroes beside your content would disgrace the past. The work and profits of the best labor system ever established have been written on these pages—the past was brilliant but the future is dismal, gloomy."

How true were these expectations from the standpoint of the Davis family is amply indicated by the scattered records kept concerning later affairs at Beaver Bend. Nothing is known precisely of what was going on between Hugh's departure and the first part of the year 1866, except that the white man Ellis remained on the job, that several parts of the plantation were rented out to white share-croppers, and that the 1865 cotton crop amounted to seventeen bales weighing 9,300 pounds. On January 1, 1866, however, Hugh's younger brother, Albert, assumed charge of the place. As described by the latter, he "went to Marion to see Mr. Tutt about hiring hands—we agreed upon general outlines & he hired me to superintend the plantation business for our Estate and directed me to complete & go ahead with the con-tract." Albert Davis, who was only twenty years of age, was faced with a tremendous task. He had to bring order from chaos; he had a "big plantation & no niggers," although, as explained, "some freedmen have promised nevertheless to feed my stock until I could make other arrangements." The next day he continued, "Struck off my contract & opened up for laborers paying from 12 dollars [a month] down according to merit—have five names signed & ready to commence work tomorrow—all of my old hands except a very few are leaving or about to leave." On the third, hands were "coming in & signing freely, Some full of fare promises & whiskey." They were put to work shelling corn, hauling wood, making axe handles, and "fixing up tools for work." By the fourth he had thirty-two hands, explaining "I have a good Stout & healthy looking set of hands & seem satisfied of keeping my crop far ahead for me to spare them part of Saturday evening [afternoon] occasionally."

Ordinary winter tasks were begun immediately, in the same manner as during the old pre-War days. The trash gang knocked down corn stalks; rice was beaten out; meat smoked; fodder stored away; wood split; and manure hauled to the fields. Repairs were made on the house in which Ellis, the white employee, was living and on the laborers' quarters. Most of the plantation animals were scattered about the country-side, but within a week it was found that at least 126 hogs were available. Fences were repaired and in the last week of January Davis recorded that "the greater part of my important fences are now in good order." Rations were issued to the Negroes "on credit at market prices." Several small plots of land were rented to white share-croppers. At the close of the month, Albert was able to report as follows on his accomplishments:

Summary for the month of January. Some of the most important items are: First hired hands & moved them in as rapidly as possible. The roads were miserable—only 7 of my old negroes would agree to live with one another—had to move most of my hands from the pararries [blackbelt] 11 & 12 miles distant. They have worked well this month. I did not get my whole force started or ready to start until the 8th of January which day I had about the largest no. out of any other day this year. Wood Cocke's old hands brot the measles here—it spread very rapidly—I have had on an average about 8 to 10 hands out from Sickness. Commenced plowing with a few of my plows on the 9th of this month—have bedded up the M. Jones Field—garden cut . . . & all of the lawn field & church field except a few acres near the circle & the little piece of fresh ground on the east side of the Church field—repaired the fence between myself & Col Morton & the fence between Pack & myslf back of the peach orchard—the greater part of the fence on the public road & from horse & hog gate to the river. Mules in only tolerable good order. 30 Sheep—139 gross [probably hogs and pigs]. Billy Hones [a Negro] killed one shoat weighing 57½. I caught him in the very act & gave him a genteel old fashioned thrashing & spared him from going to jail on condition that he would remain here until the end of the year & be a good hand—have hauled about 100 loads of manure—cut most of the logs in the fields etc etc.

For the next few months, Albert seems to have been quite successful in managing Beaver Bend. Collars of corn husks were made for the mules, corn was shelled, manure raked and spread, fruit trees trimmed, wood cut, baskets made, and rails split. By March 12, one hundred and fifty acres of corn were planted, and the Negroes were "all in fine spirits and contented to do fine work." It was admitted, however, that some of the freedmen were "growing dissatisfied" because of a short food ration and that six of them had broken their contracts. Several others had been fined for failure to carry out orders, but in general the hands were working quite satisfactorily under Albert's direction. Young Davis' last daily entry in his farm book was made on April 16, shortly after heavy rains had come to the plantation. The river had overflowed and the Negroes were put to work constructing a levee to prevent further destruction. According to Davis, "My hands men & women [thirty of them] took the mud very well—not a word of complaint was heard & men & women were both up to their ankles & knees most of the day." Despite this evidence of their willingness to work the Negroes were unsuccessful in turning out a passable cotton crop for the plantation. Picking was finished by the middle of October and only thirteen bales, weighing 6,681 pounds, were made. Such an output was exceedingly short, for 150 acres had been planted. Perhaps, however, the poor production was not the fault of the Negroes because Albert had been unable to procure new cotton seed and had planted his land in old seed which had been salvaged from the 1861-1865 crops. Since this was the case he might even be considered fortunate to have made thirteen bales.

The next available information concerning Beaver Bend is an entry made in the farm book sometime in 1871, and then it is to the effect that in 1871 the following acreages were under cultivation at the plantation: 227 acres in cotton, 171½ acres in corn, and 38 acres in oats. What was actually going on at the place between 1866 and 1871 is unknown and therefore it is impossible to describe affairs there in the years during which Reconstruction was really being felt by Alabama and the South. It is assumed, however, that throughout the period the Davises continued to operate their place, although in a very decidedly curtailed manner; and this is borne out by present-day members of the family. The family must have felt the full force of the Freedmen's Bureau, with its supervision of labor contracts for freedmen and its partial control over the Negro in politics. They were also no doubt acquainted with and hated the work of the Union League in their neighborhood. It seems quite probable, too, that Hugh and Albert were members of the Ku Klux Klan or of the Knights of the White Camelia. It is more likely that they were connected with the latter organization since the head of the order was Doctor G. P. L. Reid, a resident of Marion.[3]   The young men were staunch Democrats and worked as sincerely as any other private citizens to reestablish white supremacy in their region in the late 1860's and early 1870's.

In 1875, Albert, following the example of Hugh, Jr., abandoned the difficult task of operating Beaver Bend and moved into Marion. He was succeeded as superintendent of the plantation by his younger brother, Nathaniel, who at the time was only nineteen years of age. In December, 1869, the estate of Hugh Davis, Sr., had finally been settled, with most of the land which had formerly been cultivated at Beaver Bend becoming the property of Nathaniel.   Thus, it is with Nathaniel that the rest of this account is concerned.   It is of interest to note here, however, that at the time of the settlement of the elder Davis' estate, it was reported by administrator Tutt that the estate's receipts in cash between August 15, 1865 and December 24, 1869, had amounted to $9,473.33.   In the same period Tutt had expended the sum of $8,458.62 in payment of accounts and had advanced $1,-524.72 to the heirs.   When settlement was made the difference of $510.01 was presented to the Davises as a gift.[4]   Their annual income in the first four and a half disheartening years after the Civil War had been slightly more than two thousand dollars.

Nathaniel Davis assumed control of Beaver Bend on January 17, 1876, hiring five Negroes to work the place.   At the end of the month he described his arrangements: "Hands work four days for me for which I feed them 4 days in the week & give them 6 acres of land to be worked by my team & implements."   The next month Nathaniel bought the bond of a white man who had been convicted of adultery and sentenced by the County Probate Court to twenty-seven months of hard labor, agreed to pay the man eleven dollars a month for his work and to compensate the County for its loss of the man's work on the roads, and took him on as an extra hand.   With this white man and the five Negroes, Nathaniel set about the business of trying to make a crop.   As always, the ordinary winter work was performed and in the spring the plows were run.   Four additional hands were hired when it came time to plant corn; and throughout the year as extra help was needed to plant and clean the crops, additional Negroes were hired, usually at forty or fifty cents and board a day.   But as

[3]Walter Lynwood Fleming Papers (in possession of Judson College, Marion).
[4]Perry County, Probate Court, Minutes, M, 631-632.

was the case with other planters in Perry County in the years following the War and Reconstruction the problem of adequate labor was always severe. Davis' Negroes performed all right in the spring and summer of 1876, but when it came time to pick cotton he was forced to discharge a large portion of them for impudence, slowness, and stealing. Cotton was poor in the fall of 1876, it is true, and the hands could not be expected to pick much cotton, but even the best pickers never turned in as much as one hundred pounds a day. To solve this problem, Davis soon adopted the practice of paying his laborers on the basis of the amount of cotton picked rather than by the day. Their daily pickings then increased.

Despite the above noteworthy improvement, every time a report on affairs at the plantation was made, some statement was included concerning unsatisfactory work by the Negroes. By the end of 1876, however, the less competent hired hands had been weeded out and on December 31, Nathaniel made the following entry in his farm book: "This is the last of 1876. I can not say I have spent it as profitably as I ought, have attended to my business tolerably well, made a fair crop considering seasons. My hands have worked well and are all contented & will stay another year. Hogs have done well, two old sows, 5 shoats & 7 pigs on hand for another year. My stock have done their work well & are looking only tolerably well." He had made ten bales of cotton and had enough corn to last the next year. In 1877, his arrangements with his workers were as follows: "Jim Upshore for ½ cotton & ⅓ of corn. Tempie, Ellen & Ruth working patches for one third. John Eubanks & Frank Williams working & Deane working four days [each week]. . . . Have a good stout force who seem willing to work. Have rented Eagle Hill to John Evans for 2850 lbs. of lint—Ben Jones his land for [?]. Stephen Mosley the land he worked for 800 lbs of lint. Tena working on halves."

In 1876, Nathaniel Davis had been compelled to turn to a financial practice which finally caused him (and a large portion of the post-bellum planters) to reach near bankruptcy and to lose most of the extensive land holdings that had been inherited. Money was extremely scarce and crops were often miserable. While the modern, highly industrialized, capitalistic United States was emerging, the South was passed by; and the Southern planter despite his wide acres was gradually being ruined. Many post-bellum planters had property but few cash assets. For the most part, their fathers had invested money in two forms of wealth—land and slaves. Whenever cash had been available during the War years it had often been invested in bonds of the Confederate and state governments. Such paper was of course absolutely worthless, except for sentimental reasons, after 1865. Money which had been put into slave property was lost with Lincoln's Emancipation Proclamation and the Fourteenth Amendment of the federal constitution. Thus, land was usually the only property possessed by the post-bellum planter. Whereas he had formerly mortgaged or signed over his annual cotton crops in order to raise money, after the War he also had to mortgage his land.

Before the War, as has been shown, Southern commission merchants and factors served, at 2½ per cent commission, their planter clientale. After the War the merchants continued in business, but with a noteworthy difference in their methods. In Nathaniel Davis' case the new arrangements were as follows: a commission merchant accepted a mortgage on a piece of land; advanced a small portion of the amount in cash to the mortgagee; exacted a promise that the balance of the money called for in the mortgage be traded out with a designated merchant (frequently the mortgagor himself or a relative); allowed the planter to postpone settlement of his account either until the close of the year or at some later date; charged credit prices; tacked on to the account an interest rate up to twenty-five per cent (in the case of Nathaniel Davis); demanded the privilege of selling all cotton made by the mortgagee; exacted a high charge or commission on the sale of the bales; and soon had the planter (unless his cotton was of high quality and prices were high) so involved in debt that he often had to default on his mortgage and at times even mortgage more land to pay his account.

Because he became ensnarled in such a vicious credit system and stuck to cotton as his money crop and tried to make his white staple with a wholly unsatisfactory labor class, the Negro and white tenant and share-cropper, Nathaniel Davis' land holdings contracted almost every year. His first mortgage, for which records are available, was drawn up on March 10, 1876, when he "Fixed up papers with J. H. Burns [a merchant and money lender of Selma] for $150.00 & Drew 30.00 on account."[5] In the following years, he continued to give crop

[5]Farm Book, Mar. 10, 1876.

liens and land mortgages to Burns.   His operation of Beaver Bend
was not successful, however, and at some time between 1880 and 1895
he put into operation a steam cotton gin on his property in an effort
to supplement his income.   Even this venture was not profitable, for
in January, 1897, when all of his land except two hundred acres had
slipped away, he was forced to mortgage that piece of land as well as
his gin property.   The mortgage was for the sum of $2,592.14 and
was given to W. W. Burns of Selma.   Four years later, Davis still
owed $2,284.45 on the mortgage.   In January, 1901, his operation of
what was left of Beaver Bend was concluded.   His mortgage was due
in that month and in a last effort to salvage something from the re-
mainder of his inheritance, he deeded his two hundred acres and his
gin fixtures to John A. Fuller of Perry County in exchange for the
sum of $1,115.   Fuller also assumed responsibility for the amount still
due on the mortgage to Burns.   Davis then followed his elder brothers
to Marion, where the family turned successfully to other pursuits.
Operations of Beaver Bend by the Davis family thus came to a pitiful
end.

BIBLIOGRAPHY

Bibliographical Note

Many excellent materials on the general subject as treated in this book are available to the reader. Within the past fifteen years a literal "rebirth" in the study of Southern history has occurred and, especially until the year 1941, book-length studies on Southern subjects poured from the presses. Formal courses of the study of the history of the South were offered in the same period at approximately one hundred colleges throughout the United States. One source of information not generally employed, however, has consisted of state historical journals and magazines printed in each of the Southern states. Articles in many of those state publications have been read in the preparation of this study, although not cited except in the case of Alabama. Nevertheless, many of them have served admirably as background material, and they are highly recommended to the reader. In addition, two more widely distributed periodicals, *Agricultural History* and the *Journal of Southern History,* each of which has obtained an enviable reputation for its contents and scholarship, are particularly noteworthy for material on the subject of Southern history.

Primary Materials
Manuscripts

SAMUEL H. FOWLKES PAPERS, in possession of Edward Lee, Sylacauga, Alabama

HUGH DAVIS FARM BOOKS, in possession of Mrs. E. I. Davis and sons, Thad and N. J., Perry County, Alabama.

HUGH DAVIS PAPERS, in possession of Mrs. E. I. Davis and sons, Perry County, Alabama.

WILLIAM A. JONES PAPERS, in possession of Miss Emma Jones and Mrs. Mary J. Lowery, Perry County, Alabama.

ELISHA F. KING PAPERS, in possession of Miss Clara Barker, Marion, Alabama.

EDWIN W. KING DIARY, in possession of Mrs. Leta B. Hart, Marion, Alabama.

WALTER LYNWOOD FLEMING PAPERS, in possession of Judson College, Marion, Alabama.

Perry County, Office of Probate Court, Marion, Alabama.

Alabama Tract Book.
Deed Record.
Inventory of Estates.
Minutes, Commissioners Court.
Minutes, Orphan's Court.
Orphan's Court Register.

Record Book.
Unpublished Census Returns, 1855.
Will Book.

Printed Sources and Contemporary Accounts

FAGIN, W. L., "History of Marion, 1818-1835," *The Marion Standard*, 1909.

HAMILTON, THOMAS, *Men and Manners in America*. 2 vols. London, 1833.

JORDAN, WEYMOUTH T. (ed.), "Martin Marshall's Book: Introduction," *The Alabama Historical Quarterly* (Summer Issue, 1940), II, 158-168.

———, "Martin Marshall's Book: Household Hints," *The Alabama Historical Quarterly* (Fall Issue, 1940), II, 318-330.

———, "Martin Marshall's Book: Herb Medicine," *The Alabama Historical Quarterly* (Winter Issue, 1940), II, 443-459.

———, " 'System of Farming at Beaver Bend,' Alabama, 1862," *Journal of Southern History* (February, 1941), VII, 76-84.

———, "Martin Marshall's Book: Homemade Medicine," *The Alabama Historical Quarterly* (Spring Issue, 1941), III, 117-129.

———, "Martin Marshall's Book: Farming and Veterinary Practices," *The Alabama Historical Quarterly* (Summer Issue, 1941), III, 248-261.

———, "The Management Rules of an Alabama Black Belt Plantation, 1848-1862," *Agricultural History* (January, 1944), XVIII, 53-64.

Judson Institute Catalogue, 1844-1861. Marion, Alabama, 1844-1861.

KELLAR, HERBERT A. (ed), "A Journey Through the South in 1836: Diary of James D. Davidson," *Journal of Southern History* (August, 1935), I, 345-377.

MONETTE, JOHN W., *History of the Discovery and Settlement of the Valley of the Mississippi*. 2 vols. New York, 1846.

POSEY, WALTER BROWNLOW (ed.), "Alabama in the 1830's as Recorded by British Travellers," Birmingham-Southern College *Bulletin* (December, 1938).

TAYLOR, A. ELIZABETH, (ed), "Regulations Governing Life at the Judson Female Institute During the Decade Preceding the Civil War," *The Alabama Historical Quarterly* (Spring Issue, 1941), III, 23-29.

TOWNES, S. A., *The History of Marion, Sketches of Life, etc., in Perry County, Alabama*. Marion, 1844.

United States.
Fifteenth Census of the United States: Population.
Statutes at Large.

Secondary Materials

ABERNETHY, THOMAS PERKINS, *The Formative Period in Alabama, 1815-1828*. Montgomery, 1922.

———, *Western Lands and the American Revolution*. New York, 1937.

BABCOCK, KENDRIC CHARLES, *The Rise of American Nationality, 1811-1819*. New York, 1906.

BETTS, E. C., *Early History of Huntsville, Alabama*. Montgomery, 1916.

BONNER, JAMES C., "Plantation Architecture of the Lower South on the Eve of the Civil War," *Journal of Southern History* (August, 1945), XI, 371-388.

BOYD, MINNIE CLAIRE, *Alabama in the Fifties; a Social Study.* New York, 1931.

BREWER, W., *Alabama: Her History, Resources, War Record, and Public Men.* Montgomery, 1872.

COLE, ARTHUR CHARLES, *The Whig Party in the South.* Washington, 1913.

COLEMAN, J. WINSTON, JR., *Slavery Times in Kentucky.* Chapel Hill, 1940.

DAVENPORT, F. GARVIN, "Culture Versus Frontier in Tennessee, 1825-1850," *Journal of Southern History* (February, 1939), V, 18-33.

DAVIS, CHARLES S., *The Cotton Kingdom in Alabama.* Montgomery, 1939.

DODD, WILLIAM E., *The Cotton Kingdom.* New Haven, 1919.

FLANDERS, RALPH B., *Plantation Slavery in Georgia.* Chapel Hill, 1933.

FRY, ANNA M. GAYLE, *Memories of Old Cahaba.* Nashville, 1905.

GOVAN, THOMAS P., "Was Plantation Slavery Profitable," *Journal of Southern History* (November, 1942), VIII, 513-535.

GRAY, LEWIS CECIL, "Economic Efficiency and Competitive Advantages of Slavery under the Plantation System," *Agricultural History* (April, 1930), IV, 31-47.

———, *History of Agriculture in the Southern United States to 1860.* 2 vols. Washington, 1933.

HAMILTON, PETER J., *Colonial Mobile.* Boston, 1897.

HANSEN, MARCUS L., "The Population of American Outlying Regions in 1790," American Historical Association, Annual Report, I. Washington, 1932.

Howard College Bulletin. Birmingham, 1940.

JORDAN, WEYMOUTH T., "Early Ante-bellum Marion, Alabama: A Black Belt Town," *The Alabama Historical Quarterly* (Spring Issue, 1943), V, 12-31.

———, "The Elisha F. King Family: Planters of the Alabama Black Belt," *Agricultural History* (July, 1945), XIX, 152-162.

LLOYD, ARTHUR Y., *The Slavery Controversy.* Chapel Hill, 1939.

LYNCH, WILLIAM O., "The Westward Flow of Southern Colonists Before 1861," *Journal of Southern History* (August, 1943), IX, 303-327.

MANLY, LOUISE, *History of Judson College.* Atlanta, 1899.

MARTIN, THOMAS P., "Cotton and Wheat in Anglo-American Trade and Politics, 1846-1852," *Journal of Southern History* (August, 1935), I, 293-319.

———, "Conflicting Cotton Interests at Home and Abroad, 1848-1857," *Journal of Southern History* (May, 1941), VII, 173-194.

MITCHELL, MARTHA CAROLYN, "Health and the Medical Profession in the Lower South, 1845-1860," *Journal of Southern History* (November, 1944), X, 424-446.

MOORE, ALBERT BURTON, *History of Alabama.* University, Alabama, 1934.

———, *History of Alabama and Her People.* 3 vols. Chicago and New York, 1927.

———, "Railroad Building in Alabama During the Reconstruction Period," *Journal of Southern History* (November, 1935), I, 421-441.

OWEN, THOMAS M., *History of Alabama and Dictionary of Alabama Biography.* 4 vols. Chicago, 1921.

OWSLEY, FRANK L., "The Pattern of Migration and Settlement on the Southern Frontier," *Journal of Southern History* (May, 1945), XI, 147-176.

OWSLEY, FRANK L., and HARRIET C. OWSLEY, "The Economic Basis of Society in the Late Ante-Bellum South," *Journal of Southern History* (February, 1940), VI, 24-45.

PHILLIPS, ULRICH B., *American Negro Slavery.* New York, 1918.

————, History of Transportation in the Eastern Cotton Belt to 1860. New York, 1908.

————, Life and Labor in the Old South. Boston, 1929.

————, "Plantations with Slave Labor and Free," Agricultural History (January, 1938), XII, 77-95.

PICKETT, ALBERT JAMES, "The History of Alabama, and Incidentally of Georgia and Mississippi, from the Earliest Period. Sheffield, Alabama, 1896.

RUSSELL, ROBERT R., "The Economic History of Negro Slavery in the United States," Agricultural History (October, 1937), XI, 308-321.

————, "The Effects of Slavery upon Nonslaveholders in the Antebellum South," Agricultural History (April, 1941), XV, 112-126.

————, "The General Effects of Slavery upon Southern Economic Progress," Journal of Southern History (February, 1938), IV, 34-54.

STEPHENSON, WENDELL H., "Ante-Bellum New Orleans as an Agricultural Focus," Agricultural History (October, 1941), XV, 161-174.

SYDNOR, CHARLES S., Slavery in Mississippi. New York, 1933.

————, "The Southerner and the Laws," Journal of Southern History (February, 1940), VI, 3-23.

————, Benjamin L. C. Wailes, A Gentleman of the Old Natchez Region. Durham, 1938.

WILLIAMS, CLANTON W., "Early Ante-Bellum Montgomery: A Black-Belt Constituency," Journal of Southern History (November, 1941), VII, 495-525.

INDEX

Abolition Crusade, 20, 100

Account current (1850-51), 140-141

Adultery, 98

Agricultural fairs, 28

Alabama, a cotton state, 1; population, 2, 3, 4; prosperity, 5; settlement, 1-3

Alabama Journal, 17

Alabama Republican, The, 10

Alabama River, 14, 134, 135

Alabama Territory, 2

American Phrenological Journal and Miscellany, 17

Bank of England, 146

Barnett, J. A., overseer, 61

Beaver Bend, accounts, payment of, 120; acreage, 15, 148; acres under plow, 132; at beginning of Civil War, 151; at close of Civil War, 160; certain crops planted at, 39-40; cost of operation, 114, 118; described in 1876 by Nathaniel Davis, 166; during the Civil War, 151-152, 157, 158; entertainments and festivals, 19; location, 1; m a i n house, 19; mill established, 101; mortgaged, 167; plantation supplies, 116-123, 138; plows, number used, 33; purchased, 15; receipts and expenditures, during Civil War, 153, from 1865 to 1869, 165; records, 31-32, 59; rules, 28-31; sold by the Davises, 168; typical day's work, 96

Blackbelt, cotton production, 4; prosperity, 5-6

Blount and Tutt, merchants, 116

Brazelton, J. G., merchant, 118

Brown and Fowlkes, merchants, 116

Brown, W. R., merchant factor, 135

Burns, J. H., merchant, 167, 168

Burns, W. W., 168

Cahaba, 3, 14, 121, 134, 135, 142

Cahaba and Marion Railroad, 13-14, 21, 122, 134, 135

Cahaba Old Town, 3

Cahaba River, 15, 16, 37, 39

Catlin, I., 118

Cattle, 30, 125, 126, 158, 163

Centerville, 115

Chickens, 125

Cholera, 158

Civil War, general effects on Beaver Bend, 151-152; impressments, 156-157

Clay, J. B., overseer, 152, 153

Clothing, 156

"Club for the Cultivator," 27